We all know what it's like to be spiritually dry or stuck in a rut. Thankfully, Mart Green and David Bowden have written a life-changing book called *Learning to Be Loved*. This book is a compelling invitation to come to God with honesty and vulnerability, where he meets us and builds our faith and intimacy with him. Each chapter offers valuable spiritual insights and practical steps to overcome burnout, guiding us to a deeper, more authentic relationship with God. Highly recommended!

—Craig Groeschel, pastor, Life.Church;
New York Times bestselling author

Discovering that God not only loves but also likes me changed my life. In *Learning to Be Loved*, David and Mart guide us from head knowledge to a heart-transforming experience of God's love.

—Jennie Allen, *New York Times* bestselling author;
founder and visionary, Gather25 and IF:Gathering

God is always pursuing us, seeking to bless us with his love; all we need to do is receive it. What a gift!

—John C. Maxwell, bestselling author;
speaker; coach; leadership expert

Most Christians know God loves them, but if they were honest, they'd admit that this knowledge lives in their heads, not their hearts. They've memorized Scriptures that affirm how deeply God loves them, but a nagging sense of emptiness makes them doubt it's true. If this is you, *Learning to Be Loved* is the answer you have been waiting on. This book is to the heart what a sip of lemonade on a blistering hot day is to the body: a refreshing for the soul.

Gift of Rejection

Most of us struggle to believe in the depths of our hearts that we are truly seen, known, and loved by God. In *Learning to Be Loved*, David and Mart have given us an inspiring, honest, and practical guide to developing intimacy with God so we can flourish in life.

—Christine Caine, founder, A21 and Propel Women

No one is more qualified to write about intimacy with God than Mart Green. We're so excited that what we've learned from him privately will be shared with you in this extraordinary book.

—Dallas and Amanda Jenkins, creators, The Chosen

Learning to Be Loved will change how you relate to God. Combining poetic insight, biblical wisdom, and two lifetimes of personal experience, David Bowden and Mart Green shift us from understanding faith in God to experiencing personal relationship with him. They reveal how we often get in our own way by trying harder or accumulating more knowledge rather than noticing the ways God is already present in our lives and receiving his love. Inviting and inspiring, *Learning to Be Loved* will open the eyes of your heart to God's presence in your life.

—Chris Hodges, senior pastor, Church of the Highlands; author, *Out of the Cave* and *Pray First*

If we truly accepted the unfathomable depth of God's love for us—and then lived out of that love—how would it change us? I believe it would transform us in profound ways, and it would empower us to share that love with others. In *Learning to Be Loved*, David Bowden and Mart Green guide us through the biblical truths and spiritual disciplines that can help us finally and fully embrace the divine love our heavenly Father freely holds out to us.

—Jim Daly, president, Focus on the Family

LEARNING TO BE LOVED

LEARNING TO BE LOVED

THE EVERYDAY BELIEVER'S GUIDE TO A RICH RELATIONSHIP WITH GOD

DAVID BOWDEN AND MART GREEN

ZONDERVAN BOOKS

ZONDERVAN BOOKS

Learning to Be Loved
Copyright © 2024 by David Bowden and Mart Green

Published in Grand Rapids, Michigan, by Zondervan. Zondervan is a registered trademark of The Zondervan Corporation, L.L.C., a wholly owned subsidiary of HarperCollins Christian Publishing, Inc.

Requests for information should be addressed to customercare@harpercollins.com.

Zondervan titles may be purchased in bulk for educational, business, fundraising, or sales promotional use. For information, please email SpecialMarkets@Zondervan.com.

ISBN 978-0-310-36844-1 (audio)

Library of Congress Cataloging-in-Publication Data

Names: Bowden, David, 1987- author. | Green, Mart, author.
Title: Learning to be loved : the everyday believer's guide to a rich relationship with God / David Bowden and Mart Green.
Description: Grand Rapids, Michigan : Zondervan Books, [2024]
Identifiers: LCCN 2024018833 (print) | LCCN 2024018834 (ebook) | ISBN 9780310368427 (softcover) | ISBN 9780310368434 (ebook)
Subjects: LCSH: God (Christianity)—Love. | Christian life. | Spiritual life. | BISAC: RELIGION / Christian Living / Spiritual Growth | SELF-HELP / Spiritual
Classification: LCC BT140 .B688 2024 (print) | LCC BT140 (ebook) | DDC 231/.6—dc23 /eng/20240605
LC record available at https://lccn.loc.gov/2024018833
LC ebook record available at https://lccn.loc.gov/2024018834

Cover design: *James W. Hall IV*
Cover photo: *Adobe Stock / Bridgeman Images*
Interior design: *Sara Colley*

Printed in the United States of America

24 25 26 27 28 LBC 5 4 3 2 1

To my wife, Meagan, and my boys, Ezra and Eli

Thank you for teaching me Jesus' love by
ferociously and steadfastly loving me every day.

—David

To my wife, Diana, and my children, Brent and
Trang, Tyler and Kristin, Scott, Joe, and Amy

And to my grandchildren, TK, Isla, Harper,
Juniper, Winter, Cooper, Jed, Haven, Kinsley,
McCoy, Cade, Greyson, and Karis

Proud to see you aggressively pursuing
the mission to "Love God Intimately and
Live Extravagant Generosity."

—Mart

CONTENTS

PART THREE: LEARNING TO BE LOVED IN RHYTHMS OF FRIENDSHIP

PART FOUR: LEARNING TO BE LOVED BY LIVING IT OUT

PART FIVE: LEARNING TO BE LOVED THROUGH GOD IN YOU

LEARNING TO BE LOVED

An Introduction to Your Journey

I (David) was wrapping up my morning run and I was in tears. It wasn't from the effort. I was heartbroken and baffled, hurt and confused.

A worship music playlist was shuffling song after song into my earbuds. As I listened to one particular song about God running after me, I realized I just didn't believe it.

But it wasn't the song or even the thought that had my tears and legs running at the same time. It was a question that came into my mind.

David, do you believe your son loves you?

Whenever I came home from work, a run, or even a quick errand, my son, who was three at the time, would run, arms open and screaming "Daddy!" until he slammed into me in a beautiful collision. He would nuzzle in as we declared our love for each other.

When that happens, the voice in my head asked, *do you believe your son loves you?*

My answer came quickly, but not without pain. *No.* My answer was no. I did not believe my three-year-old really, truly loved me. *That's just what kids do. He'll grow out of it. He wants something. He's naive. If he really knew me, he wouldn't hug me so tight.* I could not receive that kind of love.

I kept running. I kept weeping. As I did, the voice returned to my mind. *You are not receiving my love either.* If I couldn't receive the unthrottled love of my own son, of course I would have great difficulty receiving God's even more lavish and undeserved love too. Not that he wasn't giving it. God was running after me fast and with more vigor than my three-year-old after I returned home. But I did not believe it.

I knew God loved me. At least in my head I did. I mean, he *has* to, right? But I did not have an experiential knowing of the real, running-at-full-speed love God has for me. I believed God is love, that Jesus came and died for those he loves, and even that his Spirit is moving me in love toward himself. I have been in public ministry for fifteen years. I lead a nonprofit called Spoken Gospel, whose mission is to show the good news of Jesus on every page of the Bible. I am committed to and convinced of God's love for the world.

But something clearly was missing.

My heart had not learned how to be loved by such a huge love. I couldn't accept that God just might be running after me like a star-crossed lover at the end of a rom-com. I couldn't feel God chasing me down just because he wanted to hold me. I couldn't relish the fact that God was hot on my heels pursuing me like a bachelor wooing his crush.

If God was running after me, it was because that's just who he is. It's just what he does. Maybe he feels sorry for me. Maybe he is rescuing me because he's just good. Maybe he is just over-flowing with grace and his overfilled cup happened to splash on my life.

Whatever I thought in that moment, I was struck by my sober reflection. I did not know in my heart that God truly loves me.

But this experience also opened up a desire in my heart that was not there before. I wanted to know that I was wanted by God. I wanted to feel him running after me. I wanted to revel in the unshakable and experiential knowledge of his love for me. And in spite of it all, I believed that that kind of love is possible.

THE MOST IMPORTANT JOURNEY OF YOUR LIFE

The most important thing you will ever do is learn to be loved by God. The Bible says, "God so loved the world," and "God is love." We've heard these statements before. I know God loves me, at least in my head. The problem is that, most days, I struggle to believe it. Do you?

I believe it is possible to be treasured by the ultimate treasure of the universe. I believe it is possible that the greatest pursuer in existence has determined in his heart to pursue me. I believe my feelings of being an imposter, being inadequate, and being tolerated really are lies. I believe that there is a God who not only loves me but likes me. A God who can't get me out of his head. A God who has been thinking about me for millennia, stretching back into a time before time. I believe it is possible that the God revealed in

Jesus really is who he said he is: a God who loves me so much that he died to make me his own.

What about you? Do you believe God loves you? If you know it in your mind, do you know it in your heart? Has the overwhelming reality of his love marked you and every part of your life? Do you carry the warmth and passion of his love with you?

Or do you feel condemned? Do you question where you stand with God? Do you find yourself spending more time negotiating your way out of guilt and coping yourself out of shame than you do feeling the delighted approval of your maker?

Do you want to be free from anxious thoughts, second-guessing, and a lukewarm faith? Then you, like me, need to make learning to be loved your obsession. You need to unlearn the lies you believe about how God sees you; you need to learn who you really are to the Father. You need to unlearn what you think God feels about you when you fail; you need to learn that the love God has for you is so intense and resilient that you can't discourage it by one degree.

We know God is love. The problem is we don't know how to receive that love. We have convictions, beliefs, worship songs, and doctrinal statements that all agree with the truth that God loves us deeply. But we don't know how to be loved that deeply. We know God has said *you are mine*. The problem is we don't know how to be his.

We have an intimacy problem with God. I don't mean intimacy in a romantic or physical way. I mean that we have a problem of being known by God and knowing God. We cover up, hide, pretend, and fake it. We struggle to let God into the secret, broken, sensitive places in our lives. And we block ourselves off from the deep, unbelievable, and category-breaking ways God loves us. This is our intimacy problem. We need to develop intimacy with God. We need to learn to let ourselves be known by God and explore the God who wants to be known.

This will be a journey. There's so much hurt to heal from. There are so many lies to stop believing. There's so much truth that needs to seep into the hard parts of our hearts. There is so much of God's love we need to discover. But all of us have the desperate need to learn to be loved by God.

A JOURNEY THROUGH THIN PLACES

More than fourteen hundred years ago, an Irish monk named Aidan listened to the waves lapping against the same rocks I was sitting on, desperately listening for God to speak. The rocks looked as if the island had gray bark-covered feet and was dipping its stony toes into the sea wash. A coastal breeze traveled across my face, carrying its precious cargo of mist. It felt as if I was alone there, happily lost in the ocean's bubbling cauldron.

I was in England on Holy Island, also known as Lindisfarne. One of my best friends in the world describes it as a thin place—an area where the staggering beauty of creation and centuries of monastic prayers have worn thin the barrier between heaven and earth. Since I was desperately in need of a word from God, I traveled to England to visit my friend and journey to this Holy Island and see for myself.

I was intrigued by the idea of a thin place. The closest approximation I had for it in the Bible was mountains. The ancient imagination saw God as dwelling in the heavens, among and above the stars. Humans live down here, on the lowly earth. But mountains are where heaven touches earth. They are high places, closer to God, where it is easier to commune with him. It's why so many of the most important moments in the Bible happen on mountains. They are like thin places, places where God seems more accessible.

While Holy Island may or may not have been a thin place, the concept of thin places has a lot of weight behind it. Some settings are better suited for the quiet and attention to beauty that aid us in communing with God. These places aren't magical. They don't hold more of God's presence. They are thin because distractions are minimized there. Silence is a thin place because we don't have to push through noise to think and listen. Nature is a thin place because an artificial world isn't blocking reminders of God's loveliness and creativity. Thin places make it easier to commune with God.

It's like installing a door in a house. The thicker the material, the harder it is to cut out the space needed to frame a door. It's not impossible. People do it all the time. But it's much more difficult to install a door in three feet of solid steel than in the wooden siding of a home. Think of thin places as the easiest place to install a door.

In this book, we will look at twenty thin places. These come from a collection of "gateways to intimacy" that my friend and coauthor, Mart Green, has put together over years of intimacy with Jesus. It's our conviction that each gateway or door is a way God gets into our lives to teach us his love. The best place to go looking for those doors, or to install them, is in the thin places.

As I sat on the shores of Holy Island, I experienced a thin place and heard God knocking on the door of prayer. He had been knocking all along, but the thick places I had been in made it hard for my ears to hear.

CHANGING THE DIRECTION
OF OUR JOURNEY

The doors we will seek to install in these thin places are often referred to as spiritual disciplines. The spiritual disciplines are a tricky subject. Practices such as prayer, Bible reading, fasting, and worship connect us to the God of infinite love. But for many they are also a primary source of guilt, anxiety, and feelings of falling short. Like many Christians, you may think, "I don't pray enough. I don't read my Bible enough. I basically never fast. Most of the time when I do get around to a quiet time, it feels empty or undeveloped." You may have picked up this book because you wanted to grow in these practices. If so, I'm glad you're here.

I have experienced all of these self-deprecating thoughts and all of these shameful emotions. But God has used faithful friends, good books, his revealing Word, and his guiding Spirit to help me through them. It is my hope and prayer that, in these pages, you will experience a similar freedom that leads to life-changing encounters with God and his category-breaking love for you.

One of the primary realizations behind this book has to do with the direction most of us believe the door through thin places swings open. We see the door of spiritual disciplines as the way we get to God. We move toward him. We enter his space. But really these doors swing out. They are the ways we describe how God gets to us. God uses the doors to move toward us.

This one realization fundamentally changed my experience of the spiritual disciplines and my walk with God. So much of my life was spent thinking I was the primary mover toward God, which meant I always needed to pray more, read more, worship more, give more, do more. If I wasn't experiencing God's love, it was because

I wasn't moving toward him enough. All of that changed when I realized that God was moving toward me.

It's impossible to learn love in a one-sided relationship. But so many of us think that intimacy with God is built solely, or at least mostly, on our pursuit of him. Let's make this really clear. God wants you to experience his love more than you possibly could. God is moving toward you in ways that no one has ever imagined before. God is an infinitely brilliant, endlessly energized, forever-faithful pursuer. And he is after you. If your relationship with God feels one-sided, it's because you are trying to do all the pursuing yourself.

God is relentlessly reaching out to you through the thin places of our world. He wants you to hear his voice, enjoy his creation, experience his healing, know his forgiveness, and revel in his rest. The thin places in our world exist because God has worn them thin through *his* pursuit of us. He has grooved a line in the carpet of the universe through his constant pacing on the floor out of his love for you.

Spiritual disciplines are not religious doors we walk through to get to God. They are the places in our world God has worn out to get to us.

Humanity didn't invent prayer as a means to talk to God and he happened to accommodate to our voices. Prayer exists because God is speaking. He is talking to us and wants us to be a part of the conversation. Prayer is a door God uses to move toward us.

The Bible isn't some magic book we interact with to reach the divine. It's also not the textbook God expects us to study to pass some final exam. The Bible exists because God revealed himself; he showed his people who he is and told them to write it down. The Bible is a door God uses to move toward us.

Fasting isn't a pious act of self-denial whereby we gain a little bit more of God's attention. Fasting exists because God is already holding out immeasurably more satisfying spiritual food with which he wants to satiate our deepest hunger. We fast to eat the meal God is offering. Fasting is a door God uses to move toward us.

The same is true of all the doors we will explore in this book. So I want to ask you to reorient the direction you believe the door to God swings open. It does not swing inward, so that we have to push it open and get to God. The door swings outward, as God bursts out of heaven and runs toward us in love.

Jesus says, "I stand at the door and knock. If anyone hears my voice and opens the door, I will come in to him and eat with him, and he with me" (Rev. 3:20). Coming into a home to have a meal was a sign of trust, friendship, and intimacy. And Jesus instigates all of it. Jesus comes to the door. Jesus knocks on the door. Jesus comes in. Jesus dines with us. God is moving toward us through myriad doors. The persistent knocks from his patient hand can be heard all around us, especially when we enter the thin places in our lives. What we will learn in this book is how to welcome God as our guest and how to receive his love as he enters.

PART ONE

LEARNING TO BE LOVED NO MATTER WHERE YOU ARE

God loves you. He is walking through the thin places to get to you. Before you do anything to pursue him, he is already pursuing you. Give yourself a moment to know this truth, to believe it, to learn it. If you are far from God, doubting God, or angry with God, he is still running after you. No matter where you are, you can learn to be loved. Take a breath. Know you are loved. Breathe out. Continue when you're ready.

ONE

SUFFERING

> We rejoice in our sufferings, knowing that suffering produces endurance, and endurance produces character, and character produces hope, and hope does not put us to shame, because God's love has been poured into our hearts through the Holy Spirit who has been given to us.
>
> —ROMANS 5:3-5

Unlearn: Suffering disconnects me from God's love.

Learn: Suffering can connect me to God's love.

IF GOD LOVES US, WHY DO WE SUFFER?

My wife and I struggled to get pregnant for what seemed to us a long time. After years of trying and disappointment, we got our first positive pregnancy test. My wife surprised me when I returned home from a trip with balloons in the living room that said "Daddy." We hugged, cried, and rejoiced. But when we went to the doctor, there was no baby to be found. Maybe it was a chemical pregnancy, maybe it was something worse, but our spirits were crushed.

We tried again. After a while we got another positive test. With far more fear and less unbridled celebration, we went to the doctor. This time was different. We heard the heartbeat. Tears of joy filled our eyes. I recorded the sound of that heartbeat on my phone and listened to it over and over again. We took the sonogram home and set up a white backdrop to take the first of a series of pictures mapping my wife's miraculous changes. At thirteen weeks we went to our doctor for the mandatory checkup, ready to see the growth of our baby and hear its heartbeat again. Our doctor, smiling in her bright office, got out the heartbeat monitor and moved it around on my wife's belly. Pictures of the healthy babies she delivered covered the office wall. She continued to talk as she searched for a sound. After a minute or so, her face changed and the searching became more uneasy. She told us that she needed to get a more detailed machine. As she left the room, my wife and I felt the bottom drop out of our lives. We found ourselves asking questions we really never thought we'd ask after hearing the heartbeat. What if our child is dead?

Our doctor couldn't find a heartbeat. Neither could the radiology lab downstairs. We went into the hospital that day with what we thought was a family of three and left with what we knew was a family of two.

In that moment, my wife and I had never been more present with suffering.

If God loves us, why does he allow us to suffer? If God wants to teach me the depths of his love, why would he throw me into the depths of pain and loss?

For so many of us, the obstacles keeping us from learning God's love are not a weak prayer life and a lack of Bible reading. They are the doubt, anger, and fear brought on by unanswered questions about suffering. We don't often have good answers to these hard questions, which is why we push them away and distance ourselves from our pain.

BE PRESENT WITH YOUR SUFFERING

We don't like to feel our pain. We prefer to distance ourselves from it. Sometimes that means we numb out. Not wanting to feel the pain, we cover it up. Suffering makes us want to push the discomfort down with late-night streaming, unhealthy eating, alcohol, pornography, distractions, and illusions of happiness.

Drowning out or stuffing up our feelings of pain can never provide a path through our suffering. Ignoring our pain cannot bring meaning to our suffering. Distancing ourselves from the sadness, emptiness, and questions brought on by suffering often just distances us from God and his love. Separating ourselves from our suffering keeps a part of us separated from some of the deepest parts of God.

We must be present with our suffering. Instead of numbing out or stuffing up, we need to feel it. We need to be sad, broken, confused, empty. When we feel the pain that suffering brings, we put ourselves in a position to feel God's love for us within it. Suffering creates a doorway into our hearts through which God can reach. Suffering reaches places within us otherwise unreachable in seasons of comfort and calm.

When we are present with our suffering, we are ready to be present with God in a powerful way. Because when we bring God our pain, he brings us his empathetic love.

AN EMPATHETIC LOVE

Empathy is one of the most powerful expressions of love. It is the act of someone entering into your pain, feeling it with you, and being willing to bear the burden of it alongside you. Empathy says, "I know. This is hard. Me too." Neurologists have demonstrated that empathy can even heal parts of the brain harmed by trauma. To have someone else with us who has lost the child, endured chemotherapy, or attempted suicide helps us know that we are not alone, not hopeless, and not unlovable.

But empathy has to be real. One of the worst things you can say to a suffering person is "I know what you're going through—my sister went through that too." While close to an empathetic response, it makes the person suffering feel all the more isolated, because you have not personally entered into his or her pain.

The power of empathy is what makes suffering such a unique and transformative gateway for God's love. God empathizes with our suffering. We may think that God is unable to empathize with us because he is holy and perfect, remote from our sin-sick world.

But that is exactly why God came to us in the person of Jesus—so he could suffer as we suffer. God became flesh so he could know us perfectly, and therefore love us perfectly. God does not stand far off and aloof from our suffering. He runs toward it in Jesus. His is the most qualified voice to speak the words of empathy, "I know. This is hard. Me too."

Have you ever suffered the loss of a position? Have you been brought low, humiliated through no fault of your own? So has Jesus. He is God himself, but he humbled himself to the point of becoming an infant born in a stable and raised by peasants.

Have you ever felt hunted down, as if everyone were after you for no reason? As if people would do anything to ruin your life? So has Jesus. As a child, he was forced to flee his country while all the other male children his age were hunted down and slaughtered.

Have you ever been destitute and hungry, without shelter, living in the street or in your car? So has Jesus. He was a homeless teacher, living off the kindness of others but often reduced to scrounging for whatever he could find.

Have you ever been falsely accused or maligned, the victim of a political witch hunt? So has Jesus. He was sold out by one of his closest friends, lied about in court, and sentenced to the death penalty for crimes he did not commit.

Have you ever been in serious physical pain, suffering so much that the foulest liquor would be a welcome relief if it just took the edge off? So has Jesus. He was sucker punched and bludgeoned by trained soldiers. He was tortured by thorns pressed onto his skull and whips ripping open his back. Huge metal nails were plunged through his wrists and ankles as soldiers pinned him to a wooden stake, which was raised in the air to slowly suffocate him.

God the Son endured all of this so that he can perfectly show his love for you when you endure it too. When we suffer, we are given the opportunity to experience one of the most powerful expressions of love—the empathy of God.

Jesus refused to numb out or ignore humanity's pain. He showed up for it. He entered it. Jesus is present in your pain; he suffers alongside you. When you are present to your suffering, Jesus is present with you. When you attend to your pain, you learn how empathetically Jesus' love attends to it as well. Real love suffers alongside. It comes closer when we are in pain.

MART'S STORY

Friends are one of God's greatest gifts. For nearly three decades, one of my closest friends was Andy McKamie. Our friendship started when he moved into his house at the same time we moved into ours, just fifty yards away. Andy and I started our businesses at about the same time. Our kids played together. We took a family ski trip together, traveled to see Christmas lights with our kids, had countless dinners with great conversations, and were together for twenty-six consecutive New Year's Days.

Andy was also my dentist. For the longest time I could not figure out the meaning of his customized license plate, "23PAIR." I can still remember him saying, "Mart, say it fast! 23PAIR—tooth repair."

Andy and I planned wedding-rehearsal dinners for our kids around the same time. We became grandparents at the same time and supported each other through loss. It's hard to sum up the value of a friendship. We measure it not in dollars and cents but rather in snapshots that somehow add up to something so much greater. Andy was one of God's great gifts to me. He was a partner with me through life's adventures, a faithful and trusted friend.

In January 2022, Andy became very sick with COVID. I was in Tulsa when my wife, Diana, sensed I might need to come home. When I arrived at the hospital, I was able to go to Andy's room to see him. Minutes later they called a code blue. I was in the corner of the room watching fifteen medical professionals do everything they could to revive Andy, but it was to no avail.

I know that if the tables had been turned, Andy would have been there for my last breath. None of us wants to suffer, but suffering is one of those unexpected paths that God comes running down to be close to us. Scripture tells us God is near to the brokenhearted, and I have heard many people testify that God was never closer to them than during their cancer, their grief, their loss, or their suffering.

I love what Tim Keller says about the promise of God in Isaiah 43:1–3: "The promise is not that he will remove us from the experience of suffering. No, the promise is that God will be with us, walking beside us in it."

I know that to be true. When I look back through my journals and remember so many of the hard things Diana and I have faced, I see God's fingerprints and am amazed at all he has brought us through. Suffering is never comfortable, never easy, but our good God uses it as one of his most sacred pathways to be intimate with us. Through suffering, God draws near and transforms us in ways that nothing else will do.

I'm still reminded of Andy every time I pull into our neighborhood or go to the dentist. New Year's Day isn't the same without him. I miss his encouragement and his prayers. But I have come to trust that God is good and that God is sovereign even in our suffering, because in suffering, God doesn't leave us, he comes close.

UNITED WITH JESUS IN SUFFERING

Jesus teaches that our suffering connects us to him. Our communion with Jesus both creates and is strengthened by suffering. This is why Paul connects his desire to know Jesus with his desire to share in Jesus' sufferings: "I have suffered the loss of all things and count them as rubbish, in order that I may gain Christ . . . that I may know him and the power of his resurrection, and may share his sufferings, becoming like him in his death" (Phil. 3:8–10).

Knowing Jesus, living with Jesus, and learning to be loved by Jesus means learning to be present in suffering with him. But not all suffering is the same. There is suffering that comes from living in a sin-marred world and suffering that comes from living as Jesus lived. We will look at how each of these unites us with Jesus and teaches us his love.

Suffering is a result of the brokenness of our world. A sin-marred world killed Jesus. When Jesus died on the cross, he not only bore the judgment our sins deserved but also bore all the cruelty of man, the corruption of religion, and the violence of the state. He bore the torturous plans of our spiritual enemies and the full weight of sin's cruelty.

When we suffer, whether it's due to an illness, an accident, or the malicious designs of someone else, we, too, are suffering in a sin-marred world. We are not suffering for sin the way Jesus did when he bore the judgment of God against sin. But this is what Paul has in mind when he writes, "I rejoice in my sufferings for your sake, and in my flesh I am filling up what is lacking in Christ's afflictions" (Col. 1:24). Nothing was lacking in the finished work Jesus accomplished through his afflictions on the cross. Paul is saying that he can rejoice in suffering because he is continuing

Jesus' completed work. There is still sin in the world. There is still brokenness. When we suffer from it, we can, in faith, continue to bear the burden of this sin-marred world alongside Jesus.

Being present to our suffering affords us the opportunity to suffer with Jesus. This is where the gateway to God's love opens wide to us. Jesus loved the world so much that he was willing to enter it and bear its cruelty. When we suffer, we are offered a glimpse of the world through Jesus' eyes. We are offered a chance to be united with Jesus in feeling love for our broken world the way he feels it.

To love a world that causes pain requires a category-breaking love. Yet this is the love Jesus has for our sin-marred world. When we suffer and yet maintain a love for this world and for people who may have caused our suffering, we inhabit the love of Jesus. We get to wear it, feel it, know it. Jesus' love for this world becomes our own. There is no better way of knowing Jesus' love than to have it for yourself. When you do, you will be able to see this world, other people, and yourself with the graciously loving eyes of God.

This is all the more true when we suffer for living like Jesus. When we suffer for following Jesus, we are not just enduring the passive violence of our sin-marred world or the impersonal malevolence of a corrupt individual. Suffering like Jesus is willingly saying yes to receiving the targeted hatred and malice that the world has for God. We can have no closer companionship with Jesus' love than when we suffer for our association with Jesus. Jesus said as much himself. "Greater love has no one than this, that someone lay down his life for his friends" (John 15:13). Jesus laid down his life for us. When we do the same for others, in the name of Jesus, we experience Jesus' love with personal knowledge.

When we choose the path of suffering for the sake of another, we learn the love of Jesus. When we forgive our enemies at great cost to ourselves, we learn the love of Jesus. When we go low, last, and least so that others go high, first, and greatest, we learn the love of Jesus.

When we suffer and see that our suffering joins us to Jesus, we are afforded the unearned opportunity to look to the savior of the world and say, *I know. This is hard. Me too.*

Do you need to hear these words from Jesus? Do you need to feel Jesus' empathetic love? Can you see how unified with Jesus you are in your suffering? Can you hear his broken and authentic voice in your ear say, *I know. This is hard. Me too?*

TWO

WOUNDS

Praise be to the God and Father of our Lord Jesus Christ, the Father of compassion and the God of all comfort, who comforts us in all our troubles, so that we can comfort those in any trouble with the comfort we ourselves receive from God.

–2 CORINTHIANS 1:3-4 NIV

Unlearn: Wounds close me off from receiving God's love.

Learn: Wounds can open me up to receive God's love.

LEARNING TO BE HATED

My dad was a pastor. Even when he stepped out of ministry after years of service, our family was still involved in our local church. This is what made it all the more surprising for me when he told my sister and me that he was divorcing our mom. Before long he was out of the house and had his own apartment. I'd go visit on the weekends. He'd take me out to lunch once a week. But I was so angry. I was angry for my mom, who didn't want the divorce. I was angry about the hole it left in our family. I was angry about the awkwardness, the new broken family rhythms, and the hypocrisy of a Bible-believing pastor who seemed to have no problem playing fast and loose with Jesus' teaching on marriage.

My heart was wounded. I experienced trauma.

After a while I started to ignore it. I'd ignore the feelings, the questions, and the father who caused them. I got involved in school, excelled in academics, surrounded myself with friends, and busied myself with as many fun things as I could. The wound was closing, scabbing, and scarring.

By the time I was ten years into my marriage, with two kids and a ministry of my own, I thought that the wound I'd experienced through the divorce had mostly closed up. Until I started crying on that run. My inability to receive my heavenly Father's love and my son's love was partly because of the wounds left by my father on his son. When I thought about my own sonship, I didn't think about running into my dad's arms when he came home from work, I thought about his leaving me at home. I didn't think about unconditional love, I thought about a conditional marriage. I didn't think about reveling in a father's affection, I thought about sitting in pain, confusion, and anger. This is what trauma does.

I knew that this was one of my life's worst wounds. But I also knew it had the potential to become the center of one of God's biggest blessings.

So I mustered up the courage to tell my dad what I was feeling. "I don't feel pursued by you, Dad. And it's making it hard to feel pursued by my heavenly Father." With understanding and tears of his own, my dad lovingly listened.

We even got to talk about the wounds his dad had left on him. How he felt ignored, overlooked, and unwanted by an absent and abusive father. This led to his own broken view of God's love. *If God is a loving father*, he thought, *he must be ignoring me because I sure don't feel loved.* My dad knew just how I felt because his wound looked so similar to my own. He had been hurt in a similar way, so he struggled to be loved by God in many of the same ways I struggled.

I invited my dad into this trauma because I wanted it to be healed. I wanted the deep wound that made me long for a pursuing father to become a deeper blessing when I found that I had one in God. The places we carry the most pain have the most power. They have the power to keep us from learning God's love, but they also have the power to be transformational places where we learn to experience it. That is why God wants to turn our worst wounds into his biggest blessings.

The wounds we carry, whether consciously or unconsciously, are some of the main things keeping us from receiving God's love. The emotional, spiritual, and physical traumas we have endured teach us not that we are loved but that we are in danger. They don't cause us to open up in vulnerable trust or reckless abandon. They close us up, scarring over the soft places in our hearts. So we learn to be protective and guarded, cynical and untrusting, self-conscious and self-blaming. Our wounds make us feel unsafe, unseen, and unwanted. They have taught us to believe that we are hated, not loved.

Wounds are the ongoing, often unseen, pain and trauma that suffering leaves behind. For a child attacked by a dog, the fear of animals may persist long after the bite heals. The child may come to believe that animals are unsafe and grow up to protect his home by not having any large pets. He may stay away from any friends' homes that have dogs and cross the street when a dog walker passes by. The physical suffering from the pain caused by the dog attack has healed completely, but the emotional wound is still shaping his life.

Most of us have suffered worse trauma than dog bites. Hypocrisy and abuse inflict church wounds. Bullying and cruelty leave us with wounds to our self-worth. The malice, lust, neglect, and anger in others have left us with wounds to our identities, trust, sexuality, views of God, and much more.

Our wounds shape our views of God and ourselves. Wounds have great power to influence how we live our lives. But that also means that, in their healing, they have a greater power to change our lives for the better.

My dad and I are meeting together regularly to talk about our wounds. Together we are opening the bandages, assessing the injuries, and applying the salve of God's love. The most beautiful thing for both of us is how we are experiencing our Father God's love for us as sons. The father wounds we both carried are becoming the white-hot center of how God is awakening us to his boundless, unconditional, and reckless Fatherly love.

The trauma of feeling rejected, ignored, or unwanted by our fathers has created in each of us a deeper ability to crave, enjoy, and be satisfied by the pursuing, attentive, and relentless love of God. The places we carry the most pain have the most power. God can turn our worst wounds into our biggest blessings.

GOD USES WOUNDS TO SHOW HIS LOVE

The whole story of the Bible follows this pattern. It is out of Israel's weaknesses and wounds, brokenness and battles, tears and trauma that God works his greatest acts of love.

This pattern is seen even more clearly in Jesus' death and resurrection. Jesus, the author of life, received the ultimate wound—death. The one who promised his followers eternal life entered the clutches of the grave. The one who called himself the resurrection and the life lay lifeless in a tomb.

Yet it was there in the one wound to which all wounds lead that Jesus brought the greatest healing. In his resurrection from the dead, Jesus used the dark, foreboding, inescapable mouth of the grave to put on display just how sure, resilient, and powerful his life is. The place with the most pain became the place with the most power.

Think also of the new heaven and new earth that Jesus will create when he returns. He will use this broken, sinful, pain-ridden earth to be his dwelling place. The Bible knows nothing of a second coming of Jesus in which we are teleported off the earth while our planet is destroyed. No! God will use our wounded world as the eternal locale for his healing home (Rev. 21:2–4).

God does not yank us out of our world of tears, pain, wars, homicide, dirty elections, cancer, divorce, pollution, and nuclear bombs as if to say, "Never mind all that. Let's go somewhere else." He comes to this twisted world, puts his kind hand to our tear-wet faces, dries the tears, and says, "It's okay. I live here now. I will heal all your wounds. I will make everything new."

God will use the most sin-stained planet in the galaxy to be his cosmic command center. He will move into the most run-down house in the neighborhood and make it his capital. He will use the deepest wounds to bring about the greatest healing. The place with the most pain will become the place with the most power. God can turn our worst wounds into our biggest blessings.

MART'S STORY

We all carry wounds. Some wounds come from what others have done and said to us. Others are self-inflicted. They find their source in our mistakes, in things we have done and said or failed to do.

One of my deepest wounds is the pain I caused some of my family members. The worst part is I didn't even know it. In business, I prided myself on being a trust builder, but at home I was failing to connect with the people I love most. Too often I would hear my wife's struggles or my children's problems and try to fix them. It worked in business, so why not at home?

My family would hint about this tendency. They tried to get through to me, but I didn't have ears to hear it. All of my defenses rushed forward to protect myself. I wanted to say, "That was not my intent. I'm doing the best I can. After all, I provide for you. I love you. Maybe you're too sensitive."

But as my children got married and we added more people to our tribe, I could tell we didn't have the relationships I wanted our family to have. My efforts to fix things weren't working, so we brought in a Christian coach to help. Candidly my thought was not about me but about the other members of my family: if these guys could get fixed, then we'd be great.

The coach started talking about trust and I felt very self-confident until he asked, "How would you rate yourself in emotional trust?"

What's emotional trust? I wondered. I had never heard of that.

"Do people come to you with their feelings," he asked, "especially when they're hurt or struggling? When people feel hurt, it's like they're in the bottom of a well by themselves. They don't want you to pull them out. Instead, they want you to get into the well. Go down with them. Feel their pain and acknowledge that it's real."

My heart ached and I felt embarrassed. For decades I had been trying to give my family advice from the top of the well. I wanted to pull them out, not empathize with them. But I was convicted. When I missed the mark of building emotional trust, it left a wound in their lives and a wound in mine.

When our wounds are exposed, we tend to blame, to cover and to hide, but that's not how wounds heal. In faith and vulnerability, we must bring them to Jesus like a patient shows his wounds to a wise doctor. As I dropped my defenses and opened my heart to Jesus, he began to affirm his love for me in my failure. He reminded me of his wounds, which paid for my mistakes. He also taught me that he's an emotional God. The Gospels are filled with descriptions of Jesus' feeling anger, compassion, joy, sorrow, and more. God showed me that emotions are one way we reflect his image.

Someone once said to me, "The deepest wound is where the flower grows." I believe that's true. No matter where our wounds come from, they are an open door, an invitation for God to come close. I have learned that if we stay open to God and vulnerable with our wounds, God will bring new and beautiful things to life in us and through us.

Jesus empowered me to move toward my family. It was humbling to go to them one by one, seeking to understand how I hurt them and how I could change. I wish I could say all the healing has occurred, but while trust is lost in buckets, it's won in drops. Now as I journey to repair the damage I caused, my wounds lead me back to Jesus to trust him, to rely on him, to be changed to be more like him. As Scripture says, "By his wounds we are healed" (Isa. 53:5 NIV).

ENTRUST YOUR TRAUMA TO GOD

Because an untreated wound can become infected, we have to let someone treat our wounds for them to heal. Sometimes this means bringing our traumas to a trusted professional, such as a counselor or pastor. Other times it means bringing them to family, friends, or the people who have wounded us. For me, it meant bringing my wound to my dad. It also means that I have to continue to bring it to professionals in God's Word and the human mind to progress on that journey of healing.

There is one healer, however, we must pay a visit to if we are to heal our wounds. When we bring our wounds to Jesus, we not only walk away with healing, we walk away with an experience of his love like none other.

The good news is that Jesus the healer came to us. The God of the universe came to meet us in our brokenness. The God of all healing came to touch our wounds. The Great Physician moved his mobile clinic into our neighborhood. The one whom our hurting hearts and diseased bodies needed most came to heal us. We do not have a God who is distant from our distress or removed from the pain of human existence. Christianity is the only religion in our wounded world whose God stepped into it!

When Jesus, the ultimate Doctor without Borders, came to us, he went to the wounded. He touched the leprous, healed the crippled, opened the eyes of the blind, loved the outcast, and included the excluded. Our inner and outer wounds did not repel Jesus but drew him close. It was not the able, equipped, hustling achievers Jesus called to himself. It was the weary, heavy-laden, burned out, hurt, and tired. Jesus explicitly said he did not come for those who are healthy. He came for the sick, both inside and out (Luke 5:31–32). Your wounds that you think keep Jesus at arm's length are the very things that make him run to your side. Doctors focus not on the healthy but on the sick. Jesus' love is increased toward us in our struggles and wounds "even as the heart of a father is to a child that has some loathsome disease, or as one is to a member of his body that has leprosy, he hates not the member, for it is his flesh, but the disease, and that provokes him to pity the part affected the more."[1]

You don't have to get over your wounds to get to Jesus. He wants to meet you in your wounds. Jesus wants to turn the place in your life with the most pain into the place with the most power to experience his love. Jesus wants to turn your worst wounds into your biggest blessings. You can entrust your trauma to Jesus.

Bring your wounds to Jesus. Invite him and others in. Experience love in the places of your life where you thought there was only pain.

What wound holds the most pain over you? Can you bring that wound to Jesus and ask him to make it a source of power? Can you receive the truth that he knows you and loves you even with all your wounds?

---

1. Thomas Goodwin, *The Heart of Christ* (Edinburgh: Banner of Truth, 2011), 155–56.

THREE

FEAR

For God gave us a spirit not of fear but
of power and love and self-control.

—2 TIMOTHY 1:7

Unlearn: I'm afraid of God's judgment and unafraid of his
forgiveness.

Learn: I'm unafraid of God's judgment and reverently fear his
forgiveness.

AFRAID OF GOD?

The threat of war and national extinction kept two kingdoms in the Middle East locked in tension as mortal enemies. The year was around 750 BC. The kingdom of Israel, though strong in its own right, was an easy target for the amassing might of Assyria. The Assyrians were cruel inventors of torture. They employed the sickest brutalities and committed war crimes to frighten their foes. They were the most wicked, most evil, and most deserving of swift justice. If given opportunity or excuse, Assyria would make quick work of Israel. The last thing the kingdom of Israel would want was for Assyria to flourish.

Yet this is what the God of Israel commanded his prophet Jonah to offer Assyria—an opportunity to repent and live. God knew the brutality of their war machines, but instead of putting an end to them, he sent Jonah to offer them forgiveness (Jonah 4:2). This assignment struck fear in Jonah's heart. Jonah was not only afraid to go to Assyria. Jonah was afraid that God would forgive Assyria. But really this story reveals Jonah's own fear of accepting God's forgiveness.

Jonah's greatest fear pinpointed where he needed the greatest love.

Thinking about fear as a way to learn more of God's love is counterintuitive. Most of us would probably assume that fear and love are at odds. After all, the Bible itself says, "Perfect love casts out fear" (1 John 4:18). To discover how fear can be a gateway to intimacy with God, we need to talk about the one phrase in God's Word where fear and God go hand in hand.

The Bible talks much about the "fear of God."

But how can you learn to love someone you are afraid of? How can you be intimate with someone you fear?

Depending on your view of God, you may be terrified of him. Afraid he's out to get you, hunting for your mistakes, waiting for you to slip up or step out of line so he can shut you out, bring disaster upon you, and ruin your life.

Some of us keep God at arm's length and dare not get too close or open up too much out of fear of being found out. *If God really knew me, he would want nothing to do with me. If I get too close to God, he will hurt me, like everyone else does.*

The fear of God is upheld throughout the Bible as an ideal, a good, and even a command. Proverbs tells us that the fear of God is the beginning of wisdom. The Law teaches that the fear of God leads to obedience, blessing, and life. And the prophets, pleading with a wayward Israel, called the nation to repentance by telling them to fear the Lord.

Yet this can seem like a contradictory idea to us as Christians today. After all, John teaches us that God is love and that his perfect love drives out fear. How often did Jesus tell his disciples not to be afraid? And Paul wrote that we have not been given a spirit of fear, but of power, love, and self-control.

That is because there are two kinds of fear. Fear that pushes you away and fear that draws you in. Consider the ocean and the many fears that can scare people away from it. Thalassophobia is the fear of deep or large bodies of water. Galeophobia is the fear of sharks. Some people even suffer from aquaphobia, which is the irrational fear of water itself. You can be so afraid of the ocean that you never want to get in it.

There is also a fear of the ocean that draws you in. This is a healthy fear, which recognizes the ocean for what it is—a powerful force of nature, full of mystery, beauty, and danger. Surfers do not ignore the fearful qualities of the ocean, they respect them. They know that the same force gliding their boards across a wave could crush them under that same wave in an instant. But the fear doesn't keep them away, it draws them in. They want to enter that power, explore that mystery, enjoy that beauty, and skirt that danger.

Is the ocean good? Yes. Should it be feared? Yes. Should fear of the ocean prevent you from enjoying its goodness? No.

So it is with the fear of God.

FEARLESS IN LOVE

Let's look at the famous "God is love" passage from John. John is talking about a future day of judgment (1 John 4:17). This will be a day when all people will need a covering for their sin in order to stand in the judgment (1 John 4:10). That kind of day can and does make us afraid. *What if I'm not good enough? What if I didn't do enough? What if God changes his mind about me? What if trusting in Jesus' cross isn't enough?* God's judgment rightly evokes fear.

Being afraid of God's judgment makes sense. But it is not meant to take up any space in the Christian's mind or heart. In the "God is love" passage where John writes about perfect love driving out fear, he is talking specifically about fear of judgment. "By this is love perfected with us, so that we may have confidence for the day of judgment. . . . There is no fear in love, but perfect love casts out fear. For fear has to do with punishment, and whoever fears has not been perfected in love" (1 John 4:17–18).

The first lesson fear has to teach us about God's love is that those who confess Jesus have no judgment to be afraid of. John says that when God's love is perfected in you, you will trust it so fully that fear has no place in your mind. If we perfectly know God's love for us, when we think about the day of judgment, we will know that we have nothing to be afraid of.

God is the ocean. But we cannot drown.

FEARFUL IN LOVE

If we have nothing to be afraid of, why should we still fear God? If we cannot drown in the ocean, why should we still respect its power and danger?

Psalm 130:3–4 gives us a reason to fear God that breaks most of our categories. It starts by naming our fear of judgment. "LORD, if you kept a record of our sins, who, O Lord, could ever survive?" (v. 3 NLT). If we stood before God and had to give an account of our sins, none of us would be left standing. This is the fear of judgment and it is very real.

But then the psalmist says this: "But you offer forgiveness, that we might learn to fear you" (v. 4 NLT). Apparently, there is a fear of God that comes not from fear that he will punish but from knowledge that he never will. There is a fear of God's punishment that we need to unlearn. And there is a fear of God's grace that we need to learn.

As recipients of God's incalculable forgiveness, we are in the palm of his hand, subjects of his inexhaustible mercy, beholders of his manifold grace, and recipients of the grandest act of absolution and reconciliation known to our universe. We are not afraid of punishment, but we fear so great and loving a God. Surely, such mercy will break our quid pro quo worldviews. Surely, such grace will overwhelm our comfortable sense of self-sufficiency. Surely, such forgiveness will challenge our judgmental and calculating souls. God's forgiveness stands to break every vestige of self we have built and to thrust upon us a new identity. Before such a storm of love, how can we not be afraid?

To fear God is to let the reality of his grandeur, the totality of his heart, and the offensiveness of his love so confront our small, unfeeling, reserved selves that we tremble at the prospect of meeting or becoming like this great God.

We have encountered a fearful forgiveness. Thus we live lives that look like our Forgiver's. Which sometimes means that he takes us to places we'd rather not go. Sometimes our fearful God leads us to fearful places.

MART'S STORY

We all face fears. It's human! Our emotions get heightened, we sense danger or feel alarm, and we want to shrink back. But I've learned that I get to choose how I respond to fear. Instead of being a pathway down which to run and hide, fear can be a gateway to intimacy with God.

Fear almost kept me from two of God's biggest dreams for my life. It began when I went to a meeting in Chicago, where I was asked to speak to a group of people. As a business guy, I was used to working with people one-on-one and was comfortable being the boss, but this time I was to speak to mostly strangers.

Just before I spoke, I ducked into a restroom and was dry heaving. That's how anxious I was. Everything within me wanted to hit an eject button and get out of there. But after the episode in the bathroom,

I offered a quick prayer to God. "God, I don't want to do this. I'm afraid, but I trust you." Was I afraid that I couldn't speak for a few minutes? No. I had what the Bible calls "the fear of man." It's the fear that says, "What will people think of me? Will I be accepted? Am I good enough?" Scripture calls the fear of man a trap (Prov. 29:25).

God didn't take away my nerves, but he assured me I wasn't alone. The meeting went well, maybe even a little too well. God gave me favor and the group not only received my idea, they wanted to run with it. My vision was for a national media campaign to promote the Bible called "Think about It." The only problem was they nominated me to be in charge of it! I had never done this before. Where was I going to find time for this? I had a chain of Mardel Christian and Education Supply stores to run. I still had four children at home. And what if it failed? What would they think of my idea then?

I still remember someone asked me that day how I felt about the task. "I'm scared," I told him. That night I went back to my hotel room scared to death. Before I went to bed, I told the Lord, "If this Bible still speaks, I could sure use a word tonight." And what I found was God waiting to meet me. In my fears, the Lord drew near. Four verses ministered directly to me. Proverbs 16:3 encouraged: "Commit your work to the LORD, and your plans will be established." Whew! I needed that one. The other verses reminded me of the importance of God's Word, the need for guidance, and the role of generosity.

After reading God's Word that evening, I wrote in my journal two things that I called "Holy Spirit promptings."

The first: "Someday there will be a project so big no ministry can do it by themselves; they will have to come together. It will be so big no resource partner can do it by themselves; they will have to come together. It will be so big that it will not happen unless the 'proclaimers' and the 'patrons' come together."

The second: "Someday there will be a world-class Bible museum with an IMAX theater in it."

These were not my dreams. They felt more like God's dreams, which he was sharing with me in advance. That night I just wrote them down in my journal and waited to see what God would do.

Twelve years later, both of these dreams came to life. My family became instrumental in launching the Every Tribe, Every Nation collective impact. It is a strategy to bring together the major Bible-translation organizations to finish all of the remaining Scripture translations in our lifetimes. It has been a miracle story in the making, but that collaboration has been happening since 2010.

The second impression came to pass when my brother and sister-in-law, Steve and Jackie, took on the project of building and launching the Museum of the Bible in Washington, DC. It was a double blessing in 2017 when at the grand opening of the Museum of the Bible we dedicated a room to highlight the need for Scripture translation all around the world.

I'm so glad God didn't give up on me in my fears. Instead, he came closer than I ever expected.

A FEARFUL FOLLOWING

God is on a forgiveness mission. He loves to absolve debts and reconcile debtors.

Remember Jonah? God wanted to offer radical forgiveness to the most undeserving empire on the face of the earth. And he wanted Jonah to make the offer. This threatened Jonah's life, Israel's national security, and the fate of the entire world. One message of forgiveness created thousands of legitimate fears. Jonah was afraid of God's forgiving someone he knew shouldn't be forgiven—because he had not yet accepted the undeserved forgiveness of God for himself.

His greatest fears pinpointed where he needed the greatest love. He was afraid of God's love because he so desperately needed it. He was afraid of others receiving the category-breaking love of God because he had not experienced it yet.

Fear is one of our best teachers. It quickly and unbiasedly tells us what we believe. Fear makes us confront beliefs about who we are. A fearful situation can force us to see ourselves as weak, needy, vulnerable, and frail. Fear also forces a confrontation with what we believe about God. When fear overtakes us, we realize that we see God as passive, uninvolved, malicious, or distracted. Fear gives us a window into what we believe about ourselves and God.

But fear can also pinpoint the places in our hearts where we most need the love of God.

If we are afraid of God's might, power, and justice, our fear exposes a belief that God is more angry than he is loving. We believe there is no escape for us. We believe God will not forgive us. But recognizing and owning this fear opens a door for God to step through and teach us who he is. God is dangerously forgiving, mightily merciful, and powerfully loving.

If we are afraid of being accepted, seen, and loved, our fear exposes a belief that we are too flawed to be treasured. We believe we are too broken to fix. We believe we are too ugly to love. But recognizing and owning this fear opens a door for God to step through and teach us who we truly are. Jesus sees us as entirely lovable, he has made us perfect, and he longs to receive us as his own.

Our greatest fears pinpoint where we need the greatest love.

Fears are not meant to be avoided, suppressed, or fled. Don't run away when fear, anxiety, or worry grips you. Instead, give yourself time to lean in. When you are afraid, ask yourself what you believe about yourself and about God. What lies is this fear revealing that you believe about yourself that you need to challenge with who God says you are? What lies is this fear revealing that you believe about God that you need to correct with the truth of who he is?

If we run from it, fear can drive us away from the greatest breakthroughs God has for us. But if we lean in to our fears, we can discover the lies we believe and how God's love wants to heal us with truth.

FOUR

NATURE

But ask the animals, and they will teach you, or
the birds in the sky, and they will tell you; or
speak to the earth, and it will teach you, or let the
fish in the sea inform you.

—JOB 12:7–8 NIV

Unlearn: I don't need creation to connect with my creator.
Learn: I need creation to connect with my creator.

WE WANT TO SEE GOD

We long to see the ones we love. Yet we can't see God (John 1:18; 1 Tim. 6:16). We can't lock eyes with him. We can't experience what his hugs feel like. That can make it difficult to feel his love and love him in return.

I admit that I have done the "star test" with God. I remember looking up at the night sky sometime in my early twenties and asking God to show himself to me by making a specific star twinkle on and off for a nanosecond. I wanted one little sign, one tiny glimpse of God with my waking eyes. I wanted to see even the shadow of the one I loved.

God did not flicker the cosmic light switch on a star that night. If you've ever tried something like this, maybe you had a different experience. But my guess is that the majority of people who have were as disappointed as I was.

I was looking for nature to reveal something about God that he was not trying to use nature to reveal. I wanted creation to prove the existence of its creator through a miraculous sign. The irony is that God was surrounding me with revelation of himself. I was just looking past it.

We long to see the one we love. The good news is God is not hiding from you. He wants to be found. He is constantly saying, *Look at me! I'm right here.* We just need to learn how to look.

God has saturated our sight with signs. He has built billboard after billboard advertising his beauty. The problem is most of us aren't paying attention. Our modern world has made it increasingly easy to distance ourselves from nature, while simultaneously making it harder for many to find a peaceful slice of it.

This has led us to believe we don't need creation to connect with

God. We have plenty of other avenues. But God has covered creation with what we're craving. God uses nature as a flashing arrow that points to his existence, power, character, and appearance.

Nature is a crucial way God shows us himself and his love. We need creation to connect with our creator.

SEEING GOD IN NATURE

King David, the famous king of God's people, Israel, told us what of God can be seen in creation when he wrote a song that we call Psalm 19. "The heavens declare the glory of God, and the sky above proclaims his handiwork. Day to day pours out speech, and night to night reveals knowledge" (v. 1). Clouds and stars, trees and grass, animals and atoms are all talking to us. Constantly and without prompting from us, all of these and more are saying something about God.

We long to see what we love. Psalm 19 says God reveals aspects of himself to us in creation. God uses creation to show us his glory, handiwork, and knowledge.

The Hebrew word *kabod*, often translated as *glory*, means "weight." You have surely felt the meaning of this weight when walking into a grand cathedral or eating a masterful meal or seeing an unbelievably talented individual perform a feat you previously thought impossible. You feel in awe, dumbstruck, lost for words, and baffled.

God does this endlessly in every corner of creation. Boundless galaxies and microscopic molecules, treacherous mountains and calm creeks, fearsome storms and warm spring days all have the capacity to grab our attention, drop our jaws, and leave us fumbling for an explanation. How could this beauty, strength, complexity, and solemnity have come to be? How can creation be expansive enough for a supernova but intimate enough for a gopher hole? How can the sun feel this good, the rain this refreshing, the wind this soft, and the grass this sweet? These questions and their answers are spoken by creation every moment of every day. The heavens declare the glory of God.

Creation also shows us God's handiwork. The world displays what God has made in the same way a museum displays art. At the edges of science and space, in the depths of unexplored seas and unplumbed quarks, creation says, "God made me." In the balance of the earth's axis and the fine-tuning of our solar system, creation says, "God did this." Our world is full of things that have been made. We live in an art gallery. Every day we walk past installations in the greatest museum of creativity. The sculptures of trees, the stretched canvas of the sky, and the detailed brushwork of a field cry out for us to behold the one who formed them. They call us to stop, enjoy, and revel in their composition and composer. God has hand formed countless wonders to show us his artistry.

Finally, nature reveals knowledge. On a recent hike with a friend of mine, we came to a lookout point where we could take in the view of the peak we were attempting to summit. I read aloud the beginning of Psalm 19 and we prayed for the knowledge of God. What we meant by that was that we wanted to know God. We wanted to see him in that mountain. What was it about God that he wanted to reveal to us about himself through this huge, permanent, and gorgeous mountain? Then we realized that's not what Psalm 19 primarily has in mind. The mountain in front of us does provide us with knowledge about God, as we've seen in his glory and handiwork. But more than that, the mountain provided us with a glimpse of God's knowledge. It showed us what God knows.

How was this mountain made? God knows. Where were we when he made it? God knows. How many lizards were born on the mountain this year? What's the exact number of ants that now walk along its rocks? God knows all of this and more. We didn't know any of this, of course. But God did. The mountain boasted of God's knowledge. Its rocks poured forth speech about how God formed it. Its cacti, bushes, and trees declared the brilliant mind of the one who dreamed them all up.

We long to see the God we love. Creation can begin to meet that longing. God uses it to make us feel his weighty glory. He has filled our world like an art museum, pointing us to the beautiful work of his hands. And he shows us how endless and staggering his knowledge is through the incredible things he has made. Psalm 19 is only one place the Bible teaches us how God reveals himself to us in nature. So much more could be said about how God is walking through the doorway of nature to show himself to you.

MART'S STORY

The clearest way God speaks is through his Word, but he also speaks to us through his world. Noah understood God's timing to exit the ark because of a dove. Elijah understood God's provision through ravens who brought him food in his hour of desperate need. Jesus himself received the Holy Spirit at his baptism like a dove descending from the sky.

In one unforgettable season, God taught me to pay attention to the ways he comes close to us through nature. One July morning I was out for a run, listening to the song "Holy Spirit" sung by Francesca Battistelli. I forgot to change the setting, so the song played on repeat again and again. As I listened, one white bird flew overhead so close to me that it caught my attention. I have been running for twenty years and I have never noticed a bird. One after another, five more white birds flew with me, filling the atmosphere above me as I ran. The words of the song rang out: "Come flood this place and fill the atmosphere."

A week later, I was on my daily run again. This time I was looking for birds, but instead I came across a snake in my path, which seemed like a symbol that what the Lord was doing in my life would involve spiritual warfare. As I continued running that morning, I saw many white herons in continuous flight.

These sightings put me on high alert. I became expectant of the way the Holy Spirit seemed to want to speak right to my heart. Six days later, while I was on vacation, a black crow brushed my head, landed in a tree, and turned to make that awful cawing noise at me. On another morning, as I took out the trash, I noticed hundreds of black birds flying over our house. But above them was a flock of white birds flying in the shape of an X.

Over the next few months, my nature sightings kept happening. White birds. Black crows. Snakes. Double rainbows. I didn't understand what it all meant, but my antenna was up. I called on several close friends to be praying for me.

In the fall, I was listening to a sermon about the church as the bride of Christ and had the thought that *bride* and *bird* are only one letter apart. Perhaps the white birds were a representation of the church? Soon after, I got a call from the influential pastor of a prominent church. He said their church was going to give $1 million over the next four years to support Bible translation. I was stunned.

The next day, I started my annual fast, and during that time I continued praying about that church and its role in Bible translation. On yet another run, I noticed two huge groups of white birds on Lake Overholser. A man walked out near them, and the first group of birds all flew up, looking like white paper flying all over the place. Maybe the church was waiting on someone to stir them up to finish Bible translation? A month later as I completed my fast, I could barely believe it when I received a call from another influential pastor of another prominent church. He told me that their church was going to give $250,000 per year for the next four years to fund Bible translation. I was overwhelmed and wept as he was telling this to me! The first pastor called one day before my fast, the second called four days after my fast, and both committed major pledges to the cause of Bible translation. I believe these two churches will lead the way in calling other churches to eradicate Bible poverty.

It took time for me to perceive it, but God was speaking to me in advance through nature. Psalm 19:1 says, "The heavens declare the glory of God," and so do the birds that fly through them.

HOW GOD SHOWS HIMSELF IN NATURE

God can communicate in nature however he pleases. He can overwhelm us with his beauty. Astound us with his knowledge. Or even communicate truths to our hearts.

Jesus even used nature to teach us how to handle anxiety.

Jesus said that when we are worried and anxious, we should consider birds (Matt. 6:25–26). He taught that birds don't have jobs and savings accounts. They don't plant crops and store up the excess harvest in a barn. They are in a far more dependent relationship with their world than we like to be. But Jesus says that God feeds them.

There are currently 10,824 species of birds, totaling between 50 billion and 430 billion individual birds. God knows and takes care of each of them. That means there are at least five times more birds in the world than there are people, yet God has the capacity and goodwill to care for them all.

Here's where Jesus leans in to show us his love. Unsurprisingly, Jesus tells us that we are way more valuable than a great host of birds. If God cares so much for cardinals, how much more does he care for you? He knows how he will provide for you as intimately as he knows which seeds in my bird feeder will go to which bird in my back yard.

God is intently watching over you. If you don't believe it, go look at some birds. Pay attention to the natural world so you can pay attention to God's love for you. Stop what you're doing, look outside, go for a walk, and find a bird. Look at it and consider God's love and care for it. By contrast, think of how much more he loves and cares for you—a human made in his image. When we consider how God cares for the universe, we learn how intentional and personal his care for us must be.

Jesus also teaches us to look at flowers. Jesus says that they are clothed in more beauty and splendor than a royal king. But they don't manufacture clothing, shop designer brands, or bargain hunt at the outlet mall. God clothes them in varied and spectacular splendor (Matt. 6:28–29). If God goes to such staggering lengths to clothe a field that sprouts up and withers in a season, how much more will he cover your eternal life with beauty (Matt. 6:30)?

God stunningly declares his attentive care for us in simple

things such as birds and flowers. God shows his healing love for us in the middle of anxiety, one of the most crippling mental assaults, and shows us love through nature. We just need to pay attention to it.

God wants to connect with you, show you his beauty, and prove his power. He has placed all of this in his created world. Are you paying attention to God's love in what's right in front of you?

PART TWO

LEARNING TO BE LOVED IN A FAMILY OF LOVE

God loves you. He is walking through the thin places to get to you. Before you do anything to pursue him, he is already pursuing you. Give yourself a moment to know this truth, to believe it, to learn it. God has created a family for you, a family where you can learn his love. God has placed gateways to himself within that family. He wants to meet you in this family. Take a breath. Know you are loved. Breathe out. Continue when you're ready.

FIVE

CHURCH

Then Peter came to Jesus and asked, "Lord, how many times shall I forgive my brother or sister who sins against me? Up to seven times?" Jesus answered, "I tell you, not seven times, but seventy-seven times."

—MATTHEW 18:21-22 NIV

Unlearn: I will learn God's love best in a church with no problems.

Learn: I will learn God's love best when I love people in a church with problems.

CHURCH HURT

Growing up, I watched my dad get fired as a youth pastor for political reasons. I saw my mom socially ostracized for sending us to public school instead of homeschooling us. I saw my sister bullied, abused, and rejected. I was fired from my first job at a church for taking a summer internship approved by the elders. A different church pulled missionary-committed funding for my wife and me to work in the Philippines because of the use of the word *pastor* instead of *teacher* in my final interview. As a traveling speaker, I've shared greenrooms with Christian "celebrities" who have made me cringe. I've seen spiritual manipulation of high school students from conference leaders at the highest level. I've seen racial prejudices ignored to the great hurt of family and friends. I've seen painful church splits over the most maddeningly tiny issues. Suffice it to say I have been beaten up by people in the church.

My guess is you have too.

The church may be the number one reason people say they leave Christianity. Specifically, people in the church are the real reason. Countless scandals make members feel betrayed. Infighting makes us feel unsafe. Personal hurts make us feel unloved. Countless numbers of genuinely hurt former believers have left their faith because they felt as though people in the church had little to do with a God of love.

With all the pain people within the church have caused, why should we look to it as a gateway for God's love? How is this a place where God runs after us in reckless, category-breaking affection? The answer is in the pain.

I was recently at a coffee shop when someone introduced himself to me. He used to attend my church but left when our lead pastor retired. Since then he'd visited a few other churches but was a self-proclaimed angsty college student who was having trouble finding a church he didn't have a problem with. He said, "I just haven't found a church that is perfect yet." I empathized with his frustration and search, as I had been there myself. Then I said, "There are two reasons you shouldn't be looking for a perfect church. First, you'll never find one, because they are full of imperfect, hard-to-love people. Second, if you do happen to find one that seems perfect, run. You'll never learn to obey Jesus in a church like that."

We talked about how Jesus loved the unwanted, the unexpected, and the unlovable. These are the ones considered to be the "other." Jesus loved the other. How could this college student be like Jesus if he wasn't around any of the others? His response was absolute gold. "You're dangerous," he said, before telling me he'd see me at church that Sunday.

The church is one of the primary gateways of God's love because the people in it can be so flawed. The church's imperfections are not a reason to leave or mistrust it; rather, they are meant to magnify the greatness of God's forgiveness. For every church split, God's love endures. For every broken relationship, God's compassion extends. For every leadership failure, God holds out world-offending grace.

We shouldn't be saying, "If God is a God of love, how could this be his church?" We should say in awe, "Only a God of love could have a church like this."

THE HUSBAND RUNS AFTER HIS BRIDE

God has always loved a hard-to-love people.

Throughout the story of the Bible, God pursues his people like a faithful husband running after his runaway bride. After their exodus from Egypt, God marries the Israelites, betrothing himself to them (Ex. 19:5–6; Jer. 2:2). Though they cheat on him, ignore him, and use him, God continues to extend his steadfast love through the cruelest adulteries (Hos. 11:7–8). Finally, after divorce papers have been served to him, God swears that he will make a new marriage covenant with them that can never be broken or voided (Jer. 31:31–32). This is the new covenant, or what many of our Bibles call the "New Testament," which Jesus brought. Jesus is our divine husband come in the flesh (John 3:29; Matt. 9:15). The people he calls to himself form his bride. On the cross, in his resurrection, and through the ongoing work of his Spirit, he makes this people perfect, spotless, and beautiful (Eph. 5:25–27). This bride, whom Jesus has pursued through the ages and died to purchase, is the church.

His own disciples disproved the notion that this bride can be made up of only flawless people who never offend or fall. Peter denied him. Thomas doubted him. Paul killed his earliest followers. The very moment after Jesus established this new covenant with his disciples, they started arguing among themselves over which of them was the greatest (Luke 22:24). Jesus did not look at these wishy-washy, divisive, petty followers and say, "This can't be my bride. How could I love people like this? How could I die for people like this? Let me look somewhere else." No. Jesus, the ultimate husband, loved his bride before she ever loved him. He died for a hard-to-love people.

This is the beauty of God's love. If he loved a lovable bride, we would not marvel at his love. If he perfected an already perfect bride, we would not stagger at his transformative power. God's love is made all the more alluring because of whom he loves. He loves us. He loves you. He loves the broken, messed up, imperfect, offensive, and hated. His love breaks all our categories. It is of a different caliber and kind, and it is best displayed in how he loves a hard-to-love church.

MART'S STORY

I'm a fifth-generation Christian on my mom's side, and third generation on my dad's. Growing up in my family, we didn't miss church if the doors were open.

A few years back, I left church to head straight to the Oklahoma City airport to pick up my good friend Steve Saint. At the time, Steve and I were working on two films together, a documentary called *Beyond the Gates of Splendor* and a feature-length film titled *End of the Spear*. Meetings with Steve were always intense and exhilarating. But as I waited for him, my phone rang. It was my wife, Diana. She was still at church and called to inform me that I had just been nominated to be on the pastor-search committee. Our pastor had recently left and we needed a new pastor. Diana told me my name was put forward, and she wanted to know whether I would decline or let my name stand. Just then I saw Steve walking toward me in the airport. Knowing that the congregation was waiting on my answer, I said a quick yes and hung up.

Five days later, I was reading a document that my brother had given me, and one paragraph jumped off the page: "Serving on a pastor-search committee is among the most far-reaching tasks anyone will ever embrace. Beyond question, your church will rise or fall on the quality of your pastor's leadership. . . . It is frankly unimaginable that a committee would undertake this most spiritual of tasks without embracing a deep process of prayer."

I certainly had not thought through the seriousness of the assignment I had accepted, but now I was all in and knew that prayer and fasting would be part of our way forward. As we waited on God, the Lord ministered to us again and again in creative ways. Songs, sermons, and Scripture passages seemed to align time after time.

One night I even woke up with this thought going through my mind: *Church ought to be a safe place for the hurting and a dangerous place for the healed.* The pastor-search committee really appreciated the thought, and we modified just one word before sharing it with our church family: "Church ought to be a safe place for the hurting and an adventure for the healed."

From start to finish the whole process took just less than a year, and it was not easy. There were times the members of the committee did not agree with one another and it looked as though we would never move forward. Along the way, we interviewed a pastor who had planted a church a few years before. I had a very strong sense he was going to be my next pastor. The trouble was that the others on the committee did not agree. It was confusing to me, but I prayed and waited. I felt sure the Lord would move the others on the committee to see this candidate as I did, but that didn't happen.

A few weeks later, we had moved on to consider a new candidate while I was still trying to make sense of my strong impression about the previous one. That's when I felt the Holy Spirit speak this statement to me: "Your job on the pastor-search committee is not to pick a pastor for yourself, it is to pick a pastor for the congregation."

Church is a great gift that way. We are brought into close, familial relationship with people we wouldn't pick for ourselves. Church is not an affinity group or a country club but a ragtag mix of disciples learning to obey all that Jesus commanded. In church, we get the chance to learn God's love for us by learning to love others.

In due time, we found a good pastor for the church, and after he was settled, Diana and I shared our sense of calling to join the previous candidate at his church. I have found that church is one of the rare places in the world where we are encouraged to love others we might not otherwise love and to put their interests above our own. I needed this lesson because this is what God is like: he loves the unlovely and chooses the unwanted, and he has loved and chosen me.

ONE ANOTHER THE OTHER

The New Testament is full of "one another" commands. We are commanded to bear one another's burdens, honor one another, bear with one another, forgive one another, accept one another, be patient with one another, confess our faults to one another. Sixteen times we are commanded to love one another.

Here's the interesting thing: God would not have to command us to love everyone if everyone were lovable.

We can't obey the call to forgive one another in a church with no offenses. We can't follow the instruction to bear with one another in a community with no burdens. We can't keep the command to be reconciled to one another in a group with no divisions. We can't love one another in the way Jesus has loved us in a church that is not hard to love.

Jesus said that even the worst people in the world love those who love them (Luke 6:32). Even people who want nothing to do with Jesus will love someone who benefits them in return (Luke 6:33). Jesus, on the other hand, calls us to love even our enemies (Luke 6:35). And even within the church we are commanded to infinitely forgive those who sin against us (Matt. 18:22).

The only church community where these "one another" commands can be obeyed is within a church filled with broken and difficult people. We need to love the others.

But we also need the love *of* others.

I am not the easiest person to love. My wife knows this better than anyone. I have strong opinions that I am quick to state and thoroughly defend. If you're not up for a debate, I don't recommend bringing up topics such as the best way to scramble an egg, the meaning of Romans 7, or the surpassing merits of third-wave coffee. I can be downright difficult to love.

These are silly examples, but the tendencies behind them have led to some humiliating moments in my marriage. In those moments when I see just how hard it must be to love me, I feel the most unlovable. I feel as though I'm worth giving up on. I feel as though I've run out of second chances. I feel like one of the others.

But in those moments when I know I've gone too far, said something stupid, and hurt the feelings of the person I love most in this world, my wife does something incredible. She patiently waits for me to get off my high horse and calm down. Then she gives me a hug and says with a sigh, "You crazy boy. I love you."

When we know we are hard to love, we feel the most unloved. But when we are loved in spite of how hard it is to love us, we know we must be truly loved.

The church is the divinely appointed place where Jesus followers show each other Jesus' love. I mean this literally. The church is the chosen organism for us to encounter Jesus' love for us and to love him in return. Just as a husband is one flesh with his wife, Jesus is one flesh with his church. That is why the church is also called the body of Christ. To love the church is to love Jesus. To be loved by his church is to be loved by Jesus.

The church is a physical place with physical people where we can experience Jesus' love.

When we love others and are loved by others, we experience and embody Jesus' category-breaking love.

Jesus wants us to experience how long-suffering, forgiving, and patient he is with us. The church is a community of people who are to show that long-suffering, forgiving patience to us. The body of Christ is equipped to love us when we are the hardest to love.

We are the other. But the community of Christ teaches us that though we may be unlovable sometimes, we are nevertheless deeply and unconditionally loved. Though we may be hard to forgive sometimes, we have been totally forgiven. Though we are the ones who cause others to suffer, we see a body that suffers willingly for us because we are greatly loved.

The church also helps us experience Jesus' category-breaking love by bringing us into community with people with whom we must be long-suffering, forgiving, and patient. When we run into those moments when we say, "There's no way I could forgive this person one more time for the same stupid thing!" Jesus says to us, "I will forgive you an endless amount of times for any stupid thing."

Our lack of patience with brothers and sisters reveals Jesus' infinite patience with us. Our short fuse reveals his long fuse. Our snap judgments reveal his gracious assessments. Our tendency to bail and move on reveals his commitment to stay and persevere.

The church embodies Jesus' category-breaking love. When we love the other, we join Jesus in his mission of love. There is no greater mystery or pleasure than that of being a carrier of the greatest love in the world. There is no greater gateway to God's love than your willingness to love the unlovable. Love the people in your church, community, and world and you will experience Jesus' love in a powerful new way.

The church embodies the love of Jesus. Through his bride, the husband is running toward us with his category-breaking love.

Is your church hard to love? Are you hard to love? Yet doesn't Jesus love you and your church? Jesus is teaching you his love for the broken through broken churches. Can you believe in a Jesus who loves that hard?

SIX

COMMUNION

When you enter the land that the LORD will give you as he promised, observe this ceremony. And when your children ask you, "What does this ceremony mean to you?" then tell them, "It is the Passover sacrifice to the LORD, who passed over the houses of the Israelites in Egypt and spared our homes when he struck down the Egyptians."

—EXODUS 12:25–27 NIV

Unlearn: I am passed over and forgotten by God.

Learn: Jesus is present with me and near to me, and he never forgets me.

PASSED OVER

Recently I was attending a Holy Communion service in a church from the Episcopal tradition. The church leaders had graciously allowed our team at Spoken Gospel to use their gorgeous grounds and chapel for a day of prayer and discernment. In the middle of the day, at noon, they hosted a communion service, which they invited us to join. About a dozen other parishioners gathered in the stained-glass, wood-lined chapel. The service and its surroundings were beautiful.

It was my first time taking communion in a high-church environment. Here the elements of bread and wine are served to you as you kneel at the front. I was last in line to make my way up to the altar. You could tell that our team had doubled the number of people they were used to serving at their noon service. I grabbed the last open spot on the far left side of the altar and knelt down. I received the bread with joy as the rector proclaimed the gospel over me. Then the cup began to make its way around. Starting on the side opposite from me, each kneeling brother and sister took a sip from the same silver goblet.

By the time the cup neared me, it had run out of wine from the influx of visitors. The cup was taken away just before my turn. I thought it was going to be refilled, so I knelt there alone at the altar for a good minute. No cup came. It was an accident, but it felt very strange and uncomfortable. Awkwardly, I got up and walked back to my seat in the rear of the chapel, past a congregation of staring silent faces.

I was passed over.

This is a feeling many of us have as Christians. We see the people around us having experiences of God, being called to great things, or seeming to have God's anointing to keep their lives together while ours fall apart. It's easy to feel overlooked, missed, even by accident. While others experience the intense affection and presence of God, we feel passed over.

Even if this is not your experience, there are surely seasons or even mornings when you reach out for God only to feel as if he missed the appointment. Some quiet times, Sunday services, or moments in our Bibles just feel passed over.

The good news is that communion is meant to set before us an intimate moment with Jesus that is both regular and real. It is regular because it happens again and again. It is real because of the physical way we interact with it.

It is so easy to feel passed over. It is easy to feel as though God is too big and we are too small. It is easy to feel as though Jesus has better people to hang out with than us. But the beauty of the Lord's Supper is that, in it, we see Jesus coming to us.

We often forget his love. But we can fight forgetfulness in this regular, real meal with Jesus.

PASSOVER: A MEMORY PARTY

For many people, the feeling of belonging comes from family. While not true for all, many families have rhythms of belonging. Moments in their year when they gather to reinforce their sense of togetherness and retell one another the stories that bind them together and define their identity.

Think about the family get-togethers that mark the annual rhythms of life. My family gathers for events such as Thanksgiving, Easter, Christmas, birthdays, Mother's Day, and Father's Day. At each of them, we eat way too much, laugh, reminisce, and honor the reason for which we are gathered. Each feast marks the remembrance of something we want to keep at the center of our families. At Easter we celebrate the resurrection of Jesus. On Christmas we rejoice and revel in his incarnation. On birthdays we eat cake and tell stories in celebration of someone we love. For Mother's Day and Father's Day we gather and toast to the honor of our parents.

These are memory parties. Feasts and gatherings centered around an important event to keep us from neglecting or forgetting what we value most. Feasting, gathering, and remembering have power. They involve us in a community. They tell us we are part of something.

This is what we should have in mind when we think about the story of our family meal—communion.

The Lord's Supper is related to a Jewish meal called the Passover. This meal is a celebration of remembrance. Each year, Jewish people remember how God saved them from slavery in Egypt and celebrate his love and their freedom. After centuries of oppression, God liberated his chosen people from Egypt. He gave commands and warnings to Israel's oppressors. He sent plagues to foreshadow the consequences of their violence. Finally, he freed his people with a final, devastating blow to the enslavers. The firstborn male from every family in Egypt would die. God would save the future generations of his chosen nation by putting an end to the generations of this oppressive nation. The people of Israel would not suffer the loss of their firstborns in order to show that "the LORD makes a distinction between Egypt and Israel" (Ex. 11:7). Death would visit every Egyptian household. But death would pass over every Israelite house.

As a sign of this imminent salvation, the people of God were to hold a feast in each of their homes. Households gathered their family or neighbors together until they had enough people to eat a whole lamb. At twilight every house butchered its lamb and barbecued it over an open fire. Some of the lamb's blood was taken and brushed around the front door as a sign that that house had been saved from bloodshed. The blood of the Passover lamb was their sign of salvation. As each family gathered inside, they belonged to the house of rescue.

Salvation was based on what house you belonged to.

Israel was commanded to annually repeat this giant cookout, followed by seven days of a festival. During the weeklong party, all their bread was to be flat, unleavened, as a sign of their quick escape from Egypt after the Passover. They had no time to let bread rise with yeast, so they had to prepare flat cakes for their hasty journey. The Feast of Unleavened Bread reminded them of the quick and sudden salvation that led to their escape from slavery.

After Israel's emancipation, God pleaded with them not to give up celebrating this meal every year (Deut. 16:1). Pay attention to the reason God gave for the necessity of this annual feast: "That all the days of your life you may remember the day when you came out of the land of Egypt" (Deut. 16:3). *Remember.* Remember the mercy, salvation, attention, and love of God. Celebrate God's rescue with a huge feast. Commemorate God's care with a weeklong party. Contemplate God's choice of you and your people with a huge, delicious meal. Passover was a memory party.

This shared meal reminded them of their shared identity. Each of them was part of God's people, and this meal proved it! When the lamb's meat passed their lips and the flat bread was on their tongues, they could taste, smell, and feel their inclusion in this story.

In fact, if anyone did not participate in this feast, that person was cut off from the people of God. To forget the story is to forget who you are. To lose the truth of God's love and rescue is to lose your identity.

Feasting, gathering, and remembering have power. This meal centered Israel on the love of their God, his choice of them as his people, and their inclusion in his story. Every year, this meal reminded Israel how much they were loved.

God gave Israel a memory party because, like all humans, they were so prone to forget. The generation God saved from Egypt quickly forgot God's choice of them and love for them. As they traveled away from slavery, they forgot about his care and worried he wouldn't provide. As they saw his presence on Mount Sinai, they forgot his covenant and built an idol to replace him. As they arrived at the promised land of Canaan, they forgot his power and refused to enter. For forty years this generation suffered outside God's promised blessings because they forgot their story.

So when the next generation was poised to enter the promised land, God made sure that they celebrated their memory party to remember who and whose they were.

We forget our story. We forget that we are loved beyond all reason. We forget that we are protected beyond all final harm. We forget that we are treasured beyond all riches. We forget who we are because we forget whose we are.

The beauty of the memory party is that we get a regular, real moment to remember our story. The regularity fights against our spiritual amnesia. The party remembers for us when we forget. The memory party is also real. It is tactile, in space and time. We touch, smell, and eat the story. It moves from our forgetful heads into our waking senses.

When we, like Israel, forget who and whose we are, the memory party comes to remind us. When we forget we are loved, communion reminds us that we are.

MART'S STORY

For years, I had been a fan of Steven Curtis Chapman's music. It seemed as though everybody else in America was as well. I was attending a Christian booksellers event when he sang his song "Be Still and Know," which is based on Psalm 46:10. That night I wrote in my journal, "I hope he sings a song for the *End of the Spear* movie someday."

About a year later, I was walking through the Kansas City airport when my phone rang. It was my friend Steve Saint, who was helping me with *End of the Spear*. His enthusiasm was spilling over: "Mart, I just got an email from Steven Curtis Chapman! He asked me for permission to write a song based on the five missionaries martyred in Ecuador."

A few months later I met Steven Curtis Chapman at the Westin Peachtree hotel for dinner. I was hoping to share the vision for the movie with him and invite him to write a song, but inside I felt like an excited little kid walking through the hotel with the most awarded artist in Christian music history.

When we first arrived, we went to the wrong elevator. It didn't go to the floor we wanted, which was the sixth, so we got off on the fifth floor. There were dust, tools, and half-finished projects everywhere. It was under construction. When we turned to get back on the elevator, the doors closed, and instead of a button to open them, there was just a tangled mess of wires. We went to use the staircase, but it was blocked off. Here I was, on the fifth floor of one of America's tallest hotels, alone with Steven Curtis Chapman. We wandered around for several minutes before we found a second set of stairs in a back corner. We finally found our way to the sixth floor for dinner, where Chapman was very attentive and interested as I shared my testimony and the story of why I was making this film. I found out that he'd had a vision for the movie even before he knew we were working on it.

After that meeting, Steven Curtis Chapman wrote not one song but three. But that wasn't the end. He came to the South American film premiere of *End of the Spear* and then took Steve Saint and a tribal man named Mincaye with him on one of his tours to spread their story.

I am blown away that God would give me access to this famous musician whose music means so much to millions of people. I was given one-on-one time with him, and it was all a gift.

Have you ever wanted to meet one of your heroes? We all do. We all want to get close to one we have loved from afar. When we come to communion, we receive an even greater gift. We draw nearer to Jesus in remembrance and experience something holy at his table. Communion is about remembering Jesus' being broken on the cross to pay for our sins. We remember that the veil of the temple was torn from top to bottom. We remember that Jesus became our high priest and gave us access to God. One-on-one time with God is now our portion. We can come boldly before the throne of grace and our heavenly Father welcomes us and hears our prayers. Communion is the gift of special access to God, our perfect Father, through Jesus Christ our Lord. There is no higher privilege and no greater gift.

PASSOVER AND OVER AGAIN

Jesus was celebrating Israel's Passover memory party when he introduced the meal we now call communion, or the Lord's

Supper. It was the day when the Passover lamb was butchered and all the people of Israel would feast in their homes. Jesus celebrated this meal with his disciples. The Passover meal would have been filled with the recounting of Israel's escape from Egypt. Psalms were quoted. Songs were sung. The meal was a sign of God's love through the Passover lamb and flat bread.

Everyone present at the meal knew the story and the signs and the meaning. But Jesus showed his disciples the whole story, the final sign, and the fullest meaning. He took some of the bread. Shockingly, Jesus said this bread was his body and his disciples should eat it. Then he took some wine from the table and said that it was his blood and that his disciples should drink it.

Jesus gave his people an ancient meal about an old slavery so they could celebrate a new freedom. Death would pass over them by the blood of the new Passover Lamb—Jesus. Their bonds of slavery to the power of sin would be broken. The love of Jesus for his people was fully displayed when he went to the cross and gave us the blood of the final Passover Lamb.

This is our new memory party. The Lord's Supper is the centering story for God's people. This is what tells us who we are and whose we are. This is the table where we gather, celebrate, and remember. Jesus has given us a party, a meal, and a story to help us never forget the one event that changed everything.

The meal not only reminds us of the story, it reminds us of our identity. Just as participation in Passover joined individuals in Israel to the people of God, the body and blood of Jesus join us to his body, the church. Communion tells us that we belong to God's house. We have a seat at the table. We belong.

Passover also tells us that we are not passed over. We are not overlooked, unwanted, or uninvolved. We are included. The meal proves it. When the bread passes our lips and the wine is on our tongue, we have physical proof that Jesus has included us in his story. Over and over again, we get to celebrate this meal to remind ourselves that death has passed us over, but God's love will never pass us over.

This regular, real meal with Jesus fights against our forgetfulness. When we can't remember how much Jesus loves us, he has a table prepared to show us. The Lord's Supper is a memory party. Every time we celebrate it, we are learning anew how to be loved.

Are you hungry for a meal with Jesus? He is ready to host you at his table. Do you want to know that you are never overlooked, never passed over? Come to the table and be with Jesus.

SEVEN

SONGS

Be filled with the Spirit, speaking to one another
with psalms, hymns, and songs from the Spirit.
Sing and make music from your heart to the Lord.

—EPHESIANS 5:18-19 NIV

Unlearn: I can know God's love without outwardly expressing
that love myself.
Learn: To know God's love I must outwardly express it.

EDUCATION, EXULTATION, EXALTATION

Our pastor didn't regularly do this, especially on a Sunday morning. The sermon was about our church's practice of worshiping God through song. The flow of our weekly service was changing and he was explaining why. Like a lot of churches, we sang first and listened to a sermon second. Though we'd often have a song or two after the sermon, the extended time of worship for our gathered church body was always before the preached Word. That was changing.

Our pastor talked about three words: *education*, *exultation*, and *exaltation*. Education is learning the Word of God. Exultation is the feelings of awe, gratitude, love, and conviction that come from learning the Word of God. Finally, exaltation is the expression of those feelings to God in song. We learn. We feel. We praise.

But our service didn't follow this pattern. We sang, started to feel, then sat down and learned. By the time our feelings were responding to God's Word, it was time to go. That was changing. From that day forward we would learn from the preached Word, have our affection stirred by what was taught, then bubble those affections out in praise through song.

As his teaching ended and we prepared to sing, our pastor did something unusual for him. He called out a specific bad habit in our congregation. With love in his voice and tears in his eyes, he admitted that a good number of people came to church late so that they skipped the singing and could just be present for the preaching. He didn't only notice this tendency. People had confessed it to him. The reason they all gave was not that they slept in or wanted a shorter service. They skipped the singing because it made them emotionally uncomfortable. It was too vulnerable to sing to God, too honest, too exposing. Others said they didn't connect with the outward, heart-led position of worship and preferred the inward, head-based practice of learning.

Many of us believe that we can know God's love without outwardly expressing that love ourselves. But for God's love to be known, it must be outwardly expressed. We must worship God so our hearts can experience the love our heads already know.

You may have your own reservations about worshiping God through song. Many don't like singing. Others don't like the style of music. Some feel as if they, or others, are faking it when they worship. Maybe you feel alone and full of doubt when you worship. Maybe seeing the conviction and joy in others only highlights the doubts and fears in your own heart. Maybe you've seen the emotional force of worship times abused into manipulation. Maybe you come from a tradition where worship is dry, boring, and void of life. While many people have a great passion for worshiping God in song, others find it difficult. This was obviously the case in my home church.

With the new structure of our services, our pastor saw that many members might now leave the service after the sermon. His concern was not that the worship band would be offended or that an exodus of members might look bad. He was concerned for the people.

This man had a PhD, wrote biblical commentaries, and preached verse by verse through the Bible. No one was more "heady" and logical than him. But he knew that education was not enough. Head knowledge puffs up the hearer until it grows old and stagnates. We must internalize what we learn, feel it, know it for ourselves. Yet, if it stops there, it is no better than lighting a candle only to suffocate it under a bowl. Outward expression of the inward experience incorporates our learning into our lives. Singing has the power to move the truth from something we know into who we are.

May I kindly and with love, as my pastor did for our church, invite you not to skip out on singing. Don't write it off or skip to a different chapter. Learn how to take the love your head knows about God and drill it into your heart.

SCREAMING ON A ROLLER COASTER

Have you ever been to a silent football game? What about a noiseless birthday party? Has a packed roller coaster ever gone downhill with no one making a sound? Of course not. Cheering at a football game or screaming over a bad call is part of the experience. The joy felt at a touchdown comes out in high fives and loud cheers. The anger felt at a game-changing ruling from the official comes out in boos and curses. When our kids blow out their birthday candles, marking another year of life, we don't sit there silently thinking how happy we are for them for finally being big enough to blow out their own candles. We clap and holler! Whether you are terrified or exhilarated on a roller coaster, you don't sit stoically. You scream from fear or delight.

Our bodies are built to express what is happening inside them.

If we don't express the thoughts and feelings we experience, we end up stifling them. Only when we outwardly manifest these inner worlds through word or deed do they integrate into the fabric of who we are.

This is why we have the expression, "It feels so good to say that out loud." You've bottled something up, and saying it changes things. It's the reason why sometimes the best thing you can do when you're sad is have a good cry. The inner knowledge of your pain and the feelings of hurt need to come out. It's why singing to your favorite song in the car brings you more joy than just listening to it quietly. It's why screaming on the roller coaster makes it more fun. We were not created to simply ponder or feel, we were created to worship. It is what we are supposed to do with all that is inside us. Worship is how we experience theology. Singing is how we experience what we know.

Eating honey teaches you more about honey than looking at it does. Walking through a forest gives you a view different from the one you get driving past it. Singing the truth of God and the cry of your heart does more for you than thinking about it does. Why? Because this is what they were made for. The sweetness of honey was made to be tasted. The beauty of a forest was made to be marveled at. The goodness of God has been revealed to us so that we might worship.

We must worship God so our hearts can experience the love our heads already know. Singing is the scream on the roller coaster. Worship is sobbing after a heartbreak. It is the seeing of what was hidden. It is the experience of what was known. It is the reality of what was guessed at. Worship completes what knowledge begins.

WHEN YOU CAN'T SING

I didn't hear my friend sing in church for months. He always sat right behind us. His love for worship mixed with his tone-deaf voice made his singing easy to hear. So when it stopped, the shift was palpable. But I didn't have to guess why he stopped singing. He and his wife had lost a child. It was devastating. The grief, doubt, and anger were crippling. Every Sunday when worship started, I could feel my body tense up. I knew that the goodness and faithfulness of God we were about to proclaim were ringing hollow in their questioning hearts. They couldn't sing that Jesus was their solid rock. They couldn't proclaim that in him they would never be shaken. They could not say that even in the darkness he was with them. Many Sunday mornings filled me with fear that I would only make things worse by declaring loudly truths they were wrestling with. So often I wouldn't sing either.

That changed one night in community group when my grieving friends shared their hearts. They admitted that they hadn't been singing in church. The pain in their hearts was too close and the truths in these songs were too far for them to even try. But worship had been their lifeblood through this season. Sunday-morning singing had been their favorite part of the week. Because when they couldn't bring themselves to sing the truths they needed most, the church sang those truths over them. When they couldn't confess God's goodness, the church did it for them. When they couldn't remind their own hearts that God was faithful, the church reminded them on their behalf. The church sang when they couldn't.

Often in our lives, our head knowledge of God's love falters. Truths we've stored up in our minds quake under the mighty weight of suffering, doubt, and despair. How can we outwardly express God's love when we are inwardly questioning it?

This is the beauty of congregational singing. Not only do we get to proclaim God's truths with our mouths, but we get to have them proclaimed to us. We get to hear the story of God sung with zeal and conviction even when we can't muster them up ourselves.

It's no wonder that, in one of the few times the New Testament instructs us to worship God in song, we are told to sing not just to God but to each other (Eph. 5:19). The songs of the church build us up even when we can't sing them.

To know God's love, we must outwardly express it. When we can't express it ourselves, we can still experience it. For the church worships God on our behalf so our hearts can experience the love our heads are struggling to know.

Consider also that the church is the body of Jesus. When the gathered body of Christ sings truths about God, they are singing Jesus' song. When the hurting, doubtful, and overwhelmed sit in a worship service, the Son of God sings his love over them. We can learn the love of God by hearing his church sing over us. When we can't bring ourselves to sing, we are in the perfect position to hear Jesus sing in our place.

MART'S STORY

When I was growing up, my mom was the choir director in our small church of a hundred people, and that meant my brother and sister and I were in the choir too. I was not especially musical, so in our Christmas program, I always got the speaking parts instead of the solos. There were times at church when a song touched me deeply, but I rarely listened to music outside of Sunday mornings. Even into adulthood, I would read books and listen to podcasts before turning on some music.

But when I started studying intimacy with God, I realized he made music a powerful gateway. Music touches our hearts and stirs our affections like few other things. To get more music into my life, I decided to start listening to a song a day. I quickly found songs ministering to my heart and drawing me closer to the Lord.

In a difficult season, Matthew West's song "Hard Season" put words and prayers to what I was feeling.

In a different season, when life was going well, my heart was stirred to praise God by Elevation Worship and Maverick City's song "Million Little Miracles."

In 2016, a hurricane headed toward South Carolina, the place where we were to host a major event for Bible translation. I was bummed. An entire year of planning and praying for this event was about to be lost. Hundreds of people who had arranged to attend were about to be interrupted. Plus, Bible translators around the world were about to lose the funds they depended on that we raised at this event. But that morning God met me through my song of the day. As I listened to Jason Gray's song "Thank You for Everything," the chorus repeated three times:

> If you lead me to still waters,
> if I'm caught in the hurricane,
> wherever you lead, I'm singing,
> "Thank you for everything."

What are the chances that my song of the day had the word *hurricane* in it? I don't remember ever hearing another Christian song using *hurricane*. It was a hard decision to cancel that gathering, but God showed me he was with us.

Within weeks God did a miracle. Many of the people who had planned to attend still gave financially, despite not hearing great speakers, listening to testimonies from the field, or gathering in person. God was with us even in the hurricane.

Music can carry truth from the head to the heart. It's no coincidence to me that the one man the Bible calls "a man after God's own heart" is the same man who wrote more songs to God than anyone else.

STORIES IN SONG

Do you know why stained-glass windows exist? They are, of course, beautiful, adorning church buildings with aesthetics fit for the contemplation of God's surpassing beauty. But most of them follow after the long tradition of the visual arts in church. They tell the story of God.

For most of the church's history, access to a Bible in a language you could read was impossible. Either it wasn't translated in your language, the translation wasn't printed or copied in a place you could access it, or you simply could not read anything to begin with. That is where the arts of the church came in. When people walked into a church, even if they couldn't understand anything else that was said or read, they could see the story of Jesus on the walls or windows. Statues, paintings, and stained glass all told the story of the gospel. Art communicated theology. Worship music still plays this vital role today.

Singing not only lets us experience what we know. Singing is an experience that teaches us what we should know.

Great worship music proclaims to us the story of the Bible, the good news of Jesus, and the character of God. Songs are meant to teach us. The melodies help us memorize and meditate on the truths revealed in Scripture.

Many Christians feel insecure in their knowledge of the Bible.

We feel anemic in our knowledge of God, lacking in our ability to relay his story. Others find the gospel hard to put into words or struggle to explain complex truths about things such as atonement in just a few simple phrases. This can make us feel second-class, underequipped, or just stupid. But all of these feelings are lies. You know what you need to know. Most likely, you have learned it and can repeat it through the songs of the church.

While we should never abandon our pursuit of knowing God through reading the Bible, we do not need to be full-time academics to have confidence in our knowledge of the gospel and the story of God. Let the songs you sing train your mind in the truths of Scripture. Let the words repeat to you, again and again, the story of Jesus. Let worship teach you the love of God as you learn about him through song.

When was the last time you let yourself feel God's love by embodying it in song? When was the last time you let his truth sing over you? To know God's love you must outwardly express it. How will you sing his love today?

EIGHT

STORIES

The accuser of our brothers has been thrown
down, who accuses them day and night before our
God. And they have conquered him by the blood
of the Lamb and by the word of their testimony,
for they loved not their lives even unto death.

—REVELATION 12:10-11

> **Unlearn:** My story is too unremarkable to show God's love.
> **Learn:** My story is so remarkable that it proclaims God's love.

YOUR STORY IS BEING STOLEN

A dear friend of mine had a difficult upbringing, coming from a lower-class, broken home. His dad was homeless and his mom shuffled through a series of homosexual relationships. His siblings regularly filled his home with violence and illicit activity. Now he is one of the most committed and genuine followers of Jesus I know. Everything in his life is different. His desires, habits, and preferences have shifted toward holiness. He's a different father, husband, and friend. He wants to know how Jesus wants him to act in a certain situation or how he can share Jesus with a coworker or family member. He has an amazing story.

But he didn't see it. He just saw it as his life. The way he saw it, he wasn't as bad as some of the people he grew up with. His home wasn't that broken, it's just how his parents were. And, besides, as far as he was concerned, Jesus hadn't changed his life that much. He still had his struggles and wasn't doing as well as that other Christian. Something was blinding him from the power of his story.

He didn't believe that his story was remarkable enough to prove how much God loved him. He needed to fight these lies and experience God's pursuit of him through his story. He needed to reclaim and retell his story to defeat the lies robbing him of God's love.

It's the same thing that robs us all of assurance, joy, and awe when we consider our own stories.

We are being lied to, incessantly. We are being accused, fooled, and gaslighted by the greatest liar of all time—Satan. "Satan" is not a name. "Satan" is a title. He is the *satan*, which means "accuser." His full-time job is to question who God is, who we are, and what God has done in our lives.

The Accuser wants to rob our stories of their ability to prove God's love to us.

He lies, saying that who we were before Jesus wasn't as bad as we thought. And he accuses us, saying we aren't as good as we should be now. He lessens the hold sin had on us before we met Jesus and heightens the hold sin has on us after. The Accuser twists life transformations into failed New Year's resolutions. Satan whitewashes a past full of slavery and pain into a former life we now miss. He gaslights us into thinking the biggest moves of God in our lives were really just the results of our gullibility and impulsiveness. The Accuser is whispering half-truths and re-written histories into our thoughts, chipping away at one of the most powerful forces we have—our stories.

It's time to take your story back.

THE BLOOD OF THE LAMB

At the end of the Bible's story, we see the Accuser defeated and thrown down (Rev. 12:8–10). A loud voice from heaven shouts out, in a victory cry, how Satan has been overcome. "They have conquered him by the blood of the Lamb and by the word of their testimony" (Rev. 12:11). Those who conquer the Accuser do so by the blood of Jesus and the story of their encounter with him.

Jesus' story is the most important. There has only ever been one being above all accusations—God himself. Without beginning and stretching beyond time without end, God's story is untwistable, unassailable, and unimpeachable. God is above every accusation the Accuser could lobby.

Yet this perfect God entered into our imperfect story. In the person of Jesus, the God above all accusation came to us. The Accuser tried to rewrite his story and gaslight Jesus against his own identity (Matt. 4:1–11). Even on the eve of his death, Jesus was still being tempted to change the end of his story, to doubt who he was and what God put him there to do (Matt. 26:39–41). But Jesus knew his story and Satan couldn't change it. When Jesus handed himself over to his accusers, remained silent through a sham trial, and gave up his life on the cross, he finished his story despite everything the Accuser tried to do to make him believe a different one. By willingly laying down his life, Jesus proved that he had all power over the Accuser and every one of his accusations.

Then, in Jesus' resurrection, his story was vindicated. How many times do you think Satan told Jesus there was nothing after death, resurrection was impossible, and he wasn't really the Son of God? But when Jesus rose from the dead, his testimony was proven true. Satan's accusations were broken and shown to be what they were—lies.

Jesus' story is how we conquer Satan's accusations. When he says that God could never love us, we point to the story of Jesus and say, "Look how much he loves me." When Satan says we'll never turn our lives around, we point to the resurrection of Jesus and say, "Look what God can bring out of a grave." The testimony of Jesus' story cuts Satan's accusations off at the knees. Jesus' death and resurrection give the Accuser nothing left to stand on. His craftiest insinuations sound like preschool name-calling. There's no power in his lies when we stand on Jesus' story. This is the power of story. This is how testimony teaches us the love of God.

We need to reclaim the story of Jesus in our lives. We need to let it have the power it has. The story of Jesus is more than enough to prove how much God loves us. His cross and resurrection are the best weapons we can take into the fight against the Accuser's lies.

We need to retell the story of Jesus in our lives. Repeating his story repeats God's pursuit of us at all costs. Repeating this story to our hearts, again and again, is the only thing that can defeat the lies robbing us of God's love.

That is how we conquer the Accuser: through Jesus' story.

MART'S STORY

In the 1950s, five young families went to Ecuador to share Jesus Christ with the Waodani tribe. Anthropologists recorded the Waodani as the most violent society ever studied. This savage tribe had a 60 percent homicide rate through five generations. Still, five missionary husbands, Jim Elliot, Nate Saint, Ed McCully, Pete Fleming, and Roger Youderian, attempted to contact the Waodani. On one of these attempts, the five men were speared to death by Waodani warriors. Their bodies were found downstream.

Little did these missionaries know that their testimony of dying for Christ on a beach in Ecuador would travel around the world and find a home in my heart as well. I first read about it in Elisabeth Elliot's book *Through Gates of Splendor* when I was young. In my late thirties, Diana and I were invited to a Bible-translation event in Lancaster, Pennsylvania. Unbeknownst to us, Steve Saint was one of the speakers. Steve's father, Nate Saint, was one of the five missionaries killed in 1956. When Steve spoke, he told his father's story and how the missionaries' wives and children forgave the Waodani people. Steve's aunt Rachel stayed in Ecuador to translate the Bible. Eventually, many of the tribe repented of their violent ways and turned to Jesus Christ as their lord and savior.

Then Steve said, "The man who speared my dad is here today." A small tribal man named Mincaye walked up front. I had never thought about the men who killed the missionaries. This was now forty years later, so I assumed they were all dead, but here was Mincaye standing before me. Steve put his arm around his father's murderer. They had even become friends.

Mincaye then said a line that changed my life forever: "We acted badly, badly, until they brought us God's carvings and now we walk his trail." I wept and wept.

The Waodani went from violence to peace because they heard, believed, understood, and obeyed God's Word. The anthropologists who studied this reported that it was because of God's Word that "they no longer allowed themselves to spear."

I was so moved by this story of reconciliation that I told my friend Rob Hoskins, "It will be a movie someday." Rob simply replied, "You do it." Through a series of events, including my taking multiple trips to Ecuador, God led me to produce a feature-length film and a documentary about this story.

When the documentary, *Beyond the Gates of Splendor*, was finished, we flew to Ecuador to premiere the film among the Waodani. A six-by-eight-foot screen was held up by sticks on three sides and a blowgun on the bottom. Speakers were mounted to the trees and a trail cut into the ground so that the cords could be buried and not tripped over. That afternoon it had rained and we had to take our screen down, but by showtime the weather had cleared. There were a hundred Waodani in attendance, plus thirty-five people from North America. We served the Waodani a supper of monkey soup first, and then around 8:00 p.m. we started the film. It was truly a unique premiere. Vampire bats flew around, dogs howled, large insects landed on the screen, and the movie paused about ten times. When it was done, the Waodani all said the "OO" sound that they make. When they were told that the outsiders clap when they approve of something, the entire group started to clap. After the film was over, they enjoyed popping all of the balloons.

Ten days later, we hosted all five of the original missionary wives along with their nine children for a North American premiere in Ocala, Florida. This was their first time together since 1957, and it was thrilling to receive their unanimous support for the project.

Two years later the feature film *End of the Spear* was released. God used this film in so many ways. From India I heard, "It almost seemed like *End of the Spear* was custom made for the unrest and animosity that are threatening to pull India apart." Numerous dignitaries and religious leaders attended each screening. Muslim imams, Buddhist monks, and Hindu priests, as well as mayors, members of parliament, and state functionaries, all insisted that they be given a copy. From the jungles of Brazil, I was told, "*End of the Spear* in the Amazon seems to have established that tribal people have a crucial role to play in serving God." From Cuba I heard, "*End of the Spear* has been shown twice on Cuban national television, and pirated copies are being bought and circulated around the island." One of my favorite responses was that it had been shown to three hundred men in prison in Florida. The chaplain wrote to tell me, "There has been much enlightenment and not a few tears from some of the most hardened inmates here. Many of the permanent men here have asked about getting a copy for ourselves."

Over the years, I have seen again and again that there is great power in a testimony. When we tell God's stories from one person or generation to the next, God draws near.

THE WORD OF OUR TESTIMONY

As he did with Jesus, Satan is accusing you. He wants to rob your story of power. Why? Because he knows that if you believe your story, all his lies will fall apart. If you think your story is that of a pretty good person who naively walked an aisle and now struggles with the same stuff they always struggled with, all of Satan's accusations have worked perfectly. You need to know your real story.

No matter who you are, where you're from, or what you've done, if you are a Christian I know a few things about your story. They are in the Bible. Let me tell them to you.

First, God chose to love and save you before he even created the world (Eph. 1:4). Before you were someone else's son or daughter, God decided to adopt you as his own kid (Eph. 1:5). With great care and intention God formed you (Ps. 139:13). Before you lived a single day of your life, God had beautiful plans and purposes laid out for you to walk in and enjoy (Eph. 2:10).

Before you came to know Jesus, you lived in complete darkness (Eph. 5:8). You were dead to anything that could give you life and only followed your passions. You were a slave to an unseen power—the same power accusing you and condemning you now (Eph. 2:1–3). No matter how good you lived, you never felt good enough (Rom. 7:9–24). No matter how much money or power you had, you had absolutely no future hope (Eph. 2:12).

But God loved you so much that he gave you his only Son (John 3:16). Instead of letting you die, in his great mercy he died on the cross (Eph. 5:2). When you came to believe this story, it wasn't you who chose God, but God who chose you (John 15:16). While you may still struggle with sin, Jesus never stops forgiving those he loves (1 John 2:1–2). You may not feel it now, but Jesus has made you perfect, spotless, and blameless, like a beautiful bride he can't wait to marry (Eph. 5:25–27). Though you may feel alone or abandoned, Jesus is coming soon to live with you forever and heal everything in you that's broken (Rev. 21:3–4).

This is your story. Do you believe it? Do you know that God chose you, loves you, wants you, has purposes for you, died for you, and desires to live with you forever? It is true. But the Accuser wants to cheapen it, twist it, or cast doubt upon it. As you make this story your own, Satan's accusations will likely grow louder. He will tell you that it may be true for someone else but can't be true for you. These are his lies.

It is time to reclaim your story.

When you accept that this is your story, when you know that this is who you are, Satan's lies cannot touch you. You will be able, like Jesus, to hear his craftiest whispers and stay true to the story God is telling in your life. Your story overcomes the Accuser. When the Accuser lies, saying, "This is who you are," you can point to your story and say, "You're wrong. I know who I am." When your story is rooted in Jesus' testimony, the narrative of your life becomes one of God's loving pursuit of you. Your whole life becomes framed by the plot of God's desire for you.

Do you believe your story? Do you believe you are that deeply loved? It's time to reclaim your story.

PART THREE

LEARNING TO BE LOVED IN RHYTHMS OF FRIENDSHIP

God loves you. He is walking through the thin places to get to you. Before you do anything to pursue him, he is already pursuing you. Give yourself a moment to know this truth, to believe it, to learn it. God is your friend. He wants to live in friendship with you. He wants to teach you his love in the rhythms of a friendship. Take a breath. Know you are loved. Breathe out. Continue when you're ready.

NINE

BIBLE

We all, with unveiled face, beholding the glory
of the Lord, are being transformed into the same
image from one degree of glory to another.

–2 CORINTHIANS 3:18

Unlearn: I cannot encounter God in a transformative way.
Learn: The Bible is where I can encounter Jesus and be
transformed.

AN ENCOUNTER WITH GOD

I love escape rooms. You are plopped in a themed room and given an hour to break out using a chain of clues and puzzles that eventually lead to the exit. I love the challenge, but I also love the surprise of discovery. When it seems as if you have no answers, a possible solution is revealed. Using your last shred of information, you figure out a four-digit code and punch it into a keypad, only for a secret door to fling open, revealing new information that provides the answers you've been looking for. When you start, you have no idea how to get out. But bit by bit, the room reveals the secret. You solve clue after clue as more and more of the room reveals itself. Finally, you get the last revelation of information—the code to break out.

In life, as in an escape room, we need revelation. We can't make sense of the mysteries, purposes, and design of our world, minds, and universe. We need answers to the questions we can't solve. Why are we here? How did we get here? What is right and wrong? Who is God? We cannot answer these questions any more than I can break out of an escape room without solving the puzzles. We need the answers to be revealed. We need revelation.

The Bible is revelation. It reveals to us who God is. Without revelation, we wouldn't know God. But through God's revelation of himself through the Bible, we can know him. We can understand his character, will, desires, actions, plans, and heart. We can see how to partner with him, be in relationship with him, and live well in the world he made. The greatest revelation God has given us is in the person of Jesus. Jesus is God himself. He is the very image of God and the exact imprint of his nature (Heb. 1:3). The best way we come to see Jesus is through the Scriptures. Jesus made this clear in one of the most important lessons he ever gave.

THE BIBLE REVEALS JESUS

In Jesus' day, rabbis taught faithful Jews how to read the Scriptures. Jesus lived the life of a rabbi. He took students, or disciples, and taught them how to interpret the Scriptures and live their lives according to them. His last lesson on how to read Scripture may have been his most important.

In Luke 24 we read how Jesus met two of his disciples traveling back home after his crucifixion. They were devastated and confused by their rabbi's death on the cross. Like many of their fellow students, they had thought Jesus was going to overthrow their Roman oppressors and usher in a season of political and economic flourishing the likes of which they hadn't seen since King Solomon. But the leader they thought would conquer their enemies was conquered by their enemies. How could he bring victory when he was defeated? The cross seemed to say that all their good news had turned bad. They explained all of this to Jesus, having no idea that he was their resurrected rabbi.

Jesus responded to their concerns by telling them they hadn't been reading Scripture the right way (Luke 24:25). All their Scriptures, what we call the Old Testament, pointed to the fact that their savior would have to first die and then rise from the dead to bring about their deliverance (v. 26). Then Jesus gave them the ultimate Bible study. Jesus showed his disciples how the whole Bible points to him. Afterward, Jesus appeared to all his disciples and opened their minds to see how the Law, Psalms, Prophets—the whole of Scripture—are fulfilled in him (vv. 44–46).

Ever since the beginning of the world, God has been telling us the story of Jesus. Every action in history recorded by his people through the Holy Spirit has told one unified message. That message is that God loves us so much that he would give up his life to bring us to himself. The message is that the death and evil we bring into the world are not enough to keep God away. The message is that God is doing everything necessary to bring life and joy to us at great expense to himself. The message is that God is merciful, loving, long-suffering, patient, gracious, and kind. The message is that God loves us so much that he gave his only Son. The message is the gospel, the good news of Jesus.

The Bible is revelation. It reveals to us who God is. And what the Bible reveals about God is seen most clearly in Jesus. The Bible is meant to show us the face of Jesus. He is how we encounter God. The Bible reveals a God who loves the outcast, heals the sick, forgives evil, and dies to save his friends. The whole Bible leads us into an encounter with Jesus. Every book of the Bible, from Genesis to Revelation, shows us a facet of God made perfect in Jesus. Every chapter and verse shows us a different hue in the multifaceted spectrum of God's beauty, seen most clearly in Jesus.

The Bible isn't a book we learn from. It is a revelation of Jesus we encounter. God longs to reveal himself to us in the person of Jesus. He wants us to encounter him. That is why he gave us the Bible.

My life radically changed when I discovered this truth. Previously for me the Bible had been either a rule book to be followed or a theological treatise to be mastered. That led me to live a life in which my relationship with God was based solely on my performance. How well did my behavior or knowledge stack up against Scripture? The shorter I fell, the worse I felt. The better I did, the prouder I became. That's because I was seeing the God of the Bible not in Jesus but through my own misreading of Scripture.

When I learned the truth of the gospel in all of Scripture,

I started to see God as he is. He loves me because he chose me, just as he chose Abraham in Genesis. He forgives me because of Jesus' blood alone, as he forgave his people through the sacrifices outlined in Leviticus. He is leading me into an eternal promised land where I will dwell with him forever, as he led Israel into Canaan, as told in the book of Joshua.

I became so convinced of these truths that a few friends and I started a ministry called Spoken Gospel. Our mission is to help people all over the world encounter Jesus on every page of the Bible. In the first five years of our ministry, our free teaching videos showed Jesus in Scripture to people more than one hundred million times. God has taken this legalistic Pharisee who almost lost his faith in the Bible and turned him into a full-time advocate for how God's Word changes everything.

But why go all in on encountering Jesus in Scripture? Why make that the focus of our ministry and the focus of this chapter? It's because an encounter with Jesus in the pages of the Bible transforms our lives to experience his love.

MART'S STORY

During my first year in college, my dad talked about the idea of a Christian retail store. At that time, he had six Hobby Lobby stores, and he said to me, "If you come home, I'll help you get a loan." So I prayed about that and decided to go back home and start Mardel, and I told myself if I didn't do well, I could always go back to school.

But we did do very well our first year and I wondered, *Where could Mardel tithe its profits?* Diana and I had been camp directors, so initially we gave to church camp ministries. Later, I learned about Bible translation and that there were six thousand vital languages on planet Earth and Scripture hasn't been adequately translated into four thousand of them. I thought, "We sell Bibles. Wouldn't it be great to help people around the world get their Bibles?" So I decided we would use our profits to help pay for first-edition print Bibles.

After we did that for a couple of years, Dave Witmer, one of the gentlemen who worked for Wycliffe Bible Translators, said, "Mart, you're paying for the printing of these Bibles. Why don't you come and see one of the Bible-dedication ceremonies? You've just got to come!"

That sounded great to me, and so on February 5, 1998, I was on a plane to Guatemala. I was reading the sheet of paper they gave me about the Eastern Jacaltec people. It said there are thirty thousand people who speak Eastern Jacaltec, but only eight thousand of them can read. Only one thousand people who speak Eastern Jacaltec are believers, but only four hundred of them can read. I'm a business guy, so three letters are always on my mind: ROI. Return on investment! What kind of return on investment was this?

I kept reading and realized that the translators happened to be from my hometown, Oklahoma City, and that they had been in Guatemala for forty years. This couple had been down there my entire life translating God's Word for thirty thousand people, but very few of them could read. And I had just paid for all of those Bibles. Now, was that a good return on investment?

I arrived at the dedication, and it was a big ceremony. They had a colorful parade through town. Four of the Eastern Jacaltec people were there who had helped translate the Bible, some of them for forty years. One of them was Gaspar. When Gaspar went forward to get his Bible, he did something I'd never seen before. He wept openly. He had to get his handkerchief out to wipe his eyes. And I was stunned watching a man weep over his Bible, because we have a thousand different types of Bibles in our bookstores, and I've helped people find the right one for them, but no one has ever wept over it. But here was a man who had labored for forty years to have God's Word in his own language, and he saw it as a treasure.

At that same moment I felt as though the Holy Spirit prompted me. "Now, Mart, why don't you go tell Gaspar he's not a good return on investment." I was embarrassed by the way I'd felt, because I realized that everybody should have God's Word in their own language.

That night at two o'clock in the morning, having just seen Gaspar weep over his Bible, I couldn't sleep. I finally got up with my flashlight and was reading a book by Kay Arthur in which she makes a simple yet profound statement: "Being in God's Word and knowing it for yourself is the key."

I got convicted by the Lord. I pay lots of money for Bible translation. I have more than forty Bibles in my home. And yet I don't read God's Word consistently.

I think the Lord had three letters on his mind. "What kind of ROI are you? What kind of return on investment is Mart Green?" I had every advantage in the world and yet I didn't consistently read God's Word. So on February 8, at two o'clock in the morning, I made a vow to the Lord: "I'm going to get up first thing and read your Word for the rest of my life."

Through this experience, God taught me I need to add a letter: EROI. Eternal return on investment. Only three things last forever: God, his Word, and people's souls. My job is to plant seeds and trust God to cause the growth. I want to invest my life in things that will pay dividends ten thousand years from now.

More than twenty-five years ago I vowed to read God's Word daily, and that started my adventure of intimacy with God. Reading God's Word and knowing it for myself has truly been the key. It has changed my life more than anything else.

FROM ONE DEGREE OF
GLORY TO THE NEXT

One of the greatest stories of transformation in the Bible is that of Moses. He had been spending a lot of time talking with God on Mount Sinai, receiving the Ten Commandments and many laws and instructions for how to build the tabernacle. But Moses had one huge request. Moses asked God to show him his glory (Ex. 33:18). God explained that if Moses saw the full weight of God's presence, he would die. So God came up with a plan. He would put Moses behind a huge rock and he could peer through a crack in the rock as God passed a small portion of his glory by. God and Moses enacted their plan and Moses saw the back side of God's glory. It overwhelmed him. He bowed his face to the ground at the briefest sight of this sliver of God's majesty through a slit in the stone.

But Moses didn't realize that this interaction marked him. The sight changed him. When he came off the mountain, all the Israelites below were terrified at what they saw. Moses' face was shining with the very glory of God that he had seen through the crack in the rock. Moses was transformed into God's image simply by seeing God. He became what he beheld.

This is the kind of encounter and transformation we can have when we read the Bible (2 Cor. 3:12–4:6). Before you just read over that, let me say it again. We can have the same transformative encounter with God that Moses had on Mount Sinai when we read the Bible.

Since Jesus is the exact image of God (Heb. 1:3), in whom all of God's glory dwells (Col. 2:9), we see the glory of God in the face of Jesus Christ. When we behold Jesus in any passage of Scripture, we encounter the glory of God. When we encounter God's glory in Jesus, we are transformed just as Moses was—we become what we behold.

These encounters usually feel everyday and natural. I have yet to see a shining light beam out of my Bible while beholding Jesus in a passage. The Holy Spirit does this work (2 Cor. 3:17). The glory we behold is not the same outward manifestation that fades away, as it was for Moses. The glory of Jesus we behold creates an inward transformation that endures and grows (v. 3). The more we look at Jesus, the more we become like Jesus. The more we see Jesus in the Bible, the more we look like the Jesus of the Bible. We can do this again and again. When we behold Jesus in the Bible, we are transformed again and again, from one degree of his glory to another (v. 18).

What deeper friendship with Jesus could there be than becoming more and more like our friend Jesus? What more intimate way could there be to learn Jesus' love than being transformed by it over and over again?

God's Word teaches us God's love by revealing Jesus to us. All the ways he loves us, forgives us, changes us, pursues us, longs to dwell with us, and gives himself up for us are on display throughout the Bible. A smorgasbord of God's love for us in Christ appears on every page of Scripture. When we realize that our Bibles contain the glory of Jesus, we will understand why Gaspar wept over his Bible in front of Mart. We will treasure it for what it is—a cleft in the rock through which we can behold Jesus and become like him.

Do you want to see the face of Jesus? Do you want to be transformed by his love? God is shining out his love for you in the story of Scripture. Can you see the Bible, not as a book you read, but as a place where you can encounter Jesus?

TEN

PRAYER

The Spirit helps us in our weakness. For we do
not know what to pray for as we ought, but the
Spirit himself intercedes for us with groanings too
deep for words.

—ROMANS 8:26

Unlearn: The quality of my relationship with God is proved by
how I talk to him in prayer.
Learn: The quality of my relationship with God is proved by
how he talks to me in prayer.

A PRAYING IMPOSTER

I was hosting a podcast series for my local church on the spiritual disciplines. When it came to the episode on prayer, our pastor hand selected three of the strongest people of prayer in our congregation. Throughout that hour-long discussion I got a glimpse into the normal prayer rhythms of these three wonderful brothers and sisters. One described how, for thirty minutes each morning, she locks herself in the bathroom to get a break from her many children. Often her time with God is so sweet that she finds herself crying with joy while sitting next to the toilet in prayer. Another talked about how she leads her children in silent moments of listening prayer. She told us stories of all the amazing truths her small kids have heard from God while lying on their living room carpet.

The stories were beautiful and inspiring, but hearing them, I felt condemned. My prayers looked nothing like theirs. I woke up early in the morning, sat for an hour in silence, and was barely able to pray a thing. Most of my prayers, once they finally got out, involved an apology for my weak prayers, a request that God would make this time feel better, and another apology for not really praying but just circling a prayer that kept eluding me.

At the bottom of it all, I felt like a fake, an imposter. I felt as though I was playing pretend. Was my heart really in this prayer? Did I really feel the loving presence of God in my breakfast nook? Did I fully, with no hesitation, believe each and every word I prayed with all my heart? I felt like a fraud.

I believed the quality of my relationship with God was proved by how I talked to him. What I needed to learn was that the quality of my relationship with God is actually proved by how he talks to me.

No other gateway has given me as much grief, doubt, and disappointment as prayer. I'm plagued with thoughts that my prayer life should be more regular, more dynamic, and more like someone else's.

Prayer is really hard for me. It's hard to get out of my head and just talk to God. It's hard to not second-guess and criticize each sentence. It's hard to try to shove the square peg of my expectations into the round hole of my experience day after day. Waking up in the morning to pray became more and more discouraging and difficult as the disappointment and disillusionment mounted. It felt like a weight I couldn't stand up under anymore.

What I needed was to stop talking and know God was speaking.

GOD IS ALREADY TALKING

I feel incredibly awkward in group settings. I'm bad at small talk. I can't chat about sports. I struggle to strike up casual conversations. If you and I were seated at a table together with a bunch of strangers, you would have to look to someone else to break the silence.

That's why I bring my wife or a friend with me when I speak at an event. They can get the conversation started when we sit at a table with strangers. They can fill the table with talking when I can't. After a while, I start to feel safer and more myself. It's then that I happily join the conversation. It's so much easier for me to join a quality conversation than to try to create a quality conversation myself.

When it comes to prayer, you don't have to start the

conversation. There is already a conversation going on. God is already at the table with you, talking. For me, I just needed to talk less so I could listen more.

God is talking to you through the indwelling Holy Spirit. All Christians are inhabited by the person of God's Spirit. There is no secret room, through some unseen door, that you have to enter to find God sitting on his throne, tapping his foot, waiting on you to finally pray. God is already within you. He is not inactive within you either. He is doing many transformative acts. One of which is praying.

God is always praying within you. Right now, the Holy Spirit is interceding for you and within you to the Father. Like me, you may not always know how to pray or what to pray, or even feel like praying. That is okay. God himself, through the Spirit, is praying for you on your behalf. This is what the apostle Paul explained to the church in Rome when they felt overwhelmed by suffering and persecution. It was hard, maybe nearly impossible, for most of them to know what or how to pray. To them and to us, he wrote, "The Spirit helps us in our weakness. For we do not know what to pray for as we ought, but the Spirit himself intercedes for us with groanings too deep for words" (Rom. 8:26).

Did you catch that? The Bible tells us that we don't know what to pray. Quality prayer is not up to our words. What freedom there is in this admission. When I admit that I don't know how to pray or what to pray for, I'm living biblically! When I struggle in prayer, I don't have to feel guilty. Instead, I can know that I am obeying the Bible. I'm living as God said I would.

My struggle with prayer doesn't disqualify me from a robust prayer life; it is actually the prerequisite. What leads to prayer that is filled with the experience of God's love and power is our admitting we don't know what we're doing and we need him to step in and do it for us.

Prayer teaches us the magnitude of God's love for us when we realize that he is always in communication with us. The Holy Spirit within you is filling in the conversational gap for you. He is already offering up great prayers on your behalf. The quality of your relationship with God is not proved by how you talk to God; it is proved by the fact that God is always talking with you.

God is always talking about us. We are always on his tongue. Our names, needs, and lives fill the conversations of the Trinity. God is talking with you and about you right now.

Prayer is listening to that conversation and knowing you are invited to join in.

How else but being in love would you describe someone who will not stop talking about you? How else but being in love would you describe someone who is always eagerly ready to listen when you're ready to talk? How else but being in love would you describe someone who is always speaking the greatest love, guidance, and wisdom into your life?

You can learn this love in prayer.

MART'S STORY

In the fall of 2007, my dad was reading something about Oral Roberts University and found out they weren't doing well in governance, leadership, and finances. Even though my dad had never gone to college, God gave him compassion for this struggling university, and he asked our family to pray about it. I thought he was crazy, but I did pray.

I also reached out to seven men in my life whom I call my "adventure partners" and asked them to pray about it too. One of them, Rob Hoskins, shared with me that just ten days before, the Lord had put an educational institution on *his* heart, and he felt I should continue to explore helping ORU out. Two others, Billy Wilson and Hal Donaldson, knew of ORU, and both encouraged me that it was worth checking into.

It was during the time of year I do an annual fast to spend more focused time seeking the Lord. One morning, just as my fast was wrapping up, I opened the newspaper to find that ORU's president had stepped down. That news felt like confirmation that I should contact them to tell them our family was interested in getting involved and to ask how we could help.

We received a call back saying that the ORU executive board wanted to meet with us. So my dad, my brother, and I drove to Tulsa. In that meeting, God gave us favor with the board as one of its leaders gave a glowing report about our family. We later shared with the entire board of ORU our intent to give financially, as well as to help recast the board with me as its chair. It was intimidating to ask forty-six board members to resign from their roles so we could build a new future for the university.

But God spoke to my mom as she was praying and gave her encouragement from Joshua 1:7: "Be strong and very courageous. Be careful to obey all the law my servant Moses gave you; do not turn from it to the right or to the left, that you may be successful wherever you go" (NIV).

"That is a promise for you, Mart," she said. She was right, and God answered our prayers. The board did resign, and my next step was to find an expert in university governance. So I prayed again, "Lord, please send me the right people. I'm in way over my head with the problems this university is facing."

Oral Roberts University had four dragons in front of it. The first was debt, $60 million worth. The second was $100 million of deferred campus maintenance. The third was a significant annual deficit, and the fourth was declining enrollment. Some were saying ORU was a sinking ship, but we believed God had other plans.

Several people told me about a man named Bob Cooley who could help with university governance. I flew to Charlotte, North Carolina, to meet with him, and Bob turned out to be a world-class guy and an incredible answer to prayer. For the next six years, he was by my side helping to reestablish good governance.

Our family committed $70 million, our largest gift ever, to kickstart a new season for ORU. God also provided me with fifteen new board members and a new president. And together we led the university in a healthy direction.

With every prayer, God was building my faith. Again and again I needed God to provide the right people at the right time. One of my main prayers in life comes from Luke 10:2: "The harvest is plentiful, but the laborers are few. Therefore pray earnestly to the Lord of the harvest to send out laborers into his harvest."

I found that prayer is an invitation to draw close to God and watch him do what only he can do.

LISTENING IS PRAYER

When Mart and his family prayed through the difficult decisions surrounding ORU, it wasn't how much they talked or what they interceded for that made the biggest differences. It was what they heard. They were listening to God's voice at every step through times of prayer.

Unlike what most of us have been taught or assumed, prayer is primarily an act of listening. Two of Jesus' main teachings on prayer emphasize this. When he gave us the brief Lord's Prayer, it was in contrast to the long, impressive, wordy prayers of the religious people of his day (Matt. 6:5–7). God loves short and simple prayers. He loves them because they express a radical trust in the fact that he knows what we need and is happy to give it to us without being convinced (v. 8). He also loves them because they leave lots of room for us to listen to his voice. This is the other side of Jesus' teaching on prayer. He often taught that God would answer our prayers if we pray in his name, which is to say in accordance with his will (John 14:13; 1 John 5:14). Praying in Jesus' name is not just slapping his name on the end of a prayer. It is meant to be a prayer that Jesus would pray, a prayer according to his will, in line with his name. How can we know God's will and pray as Jesus would pray? We listen. We listen to the prayers God is already praying through his Spirit within us. We tune in to the conversation. We pray "in the Spirit" (Eph. 6:18).

Here lies an often-untapped depth of God's love in the lives of many believers. Love is often expressed and experienced through spoken words. We call our moms because we love them, and they call us for the same reason. Cards and letters are words passed between people who share love. My wife and I say "I love you" to each other dozens of times a day because our words of love signal to each other that we are loved. We have a God who speaks with us. The God whose words created galaxies and geckos uses his words to speak directly with us. God talks to us because he loves us. Even when we can't hear him, or when we struggle to tune in to the constant conversation between Father and Spirit happening within us, knowledge of how loved we are can well up just by remembering that he is in fact speaking.

God is talking to you. The Spirit is praying within you. Jesus is interceding for you. Do you believe this? Can you base your relationship with God, not on how well you talk to him, but on how he can't stop talking about you?

ELEVEN

FASTING

O God, you are my God; earnestly I seek you;
my soul thirsts for you; my flesh faints for you, as
in a dry and weary land where there is no water.

—PSALM 63:1

Unlearn: We fast to go without and prove our devotion to God.

Learn: We fast to feast on God and enjoy his devotion to us.

FAILING TO FAST

Fasting was part of the curriculum. I was getting my master's degree in theology and the spiritual disciplines class required a fast of at least twenty-four hours with a journal reflection to follow. I had my last meal on night one and intended to eat again on the morning of the third day. That would leave one full day and night without food.

I was excited for the assignment because I really hadn't fasted that much. I was at a crucial turning point in my life and needed to hear God's voice. So I thought the fast would make his voice clear.

Skipping breakfast and lunch was easy. But by the end of the day, I hadn't heard anything. I felt as though my fast had failed. So instead of waiting until the morning, I ordered a large Papa Johns pizza and ate most of it while watching TV. Let's just say I didn't feel great about myself after that.

So many people have told me about similar experiences in their lives. They fasted but got too hungry and needed to eat. They fasted but didn't hear from God. They fasted but feel like they gave up too soon.

I also hear fasting talked about as something we do to get God's focus, show him that we are really genuine, and earn a little more attention from him than normal. The way I saw it, fasting was a spiritual key I could use to unlock a special moment with God. It was a cheat code in a video game to jump ahead a few levels.

But fasting isn't about depriving yourself of something so that God sees your effort and answers your prayers. Fasting isn't a devout bargaining chip. Fasting is not primarily about cutting off your food source; fasting is about choosing to eat different food. Fasting isn't starving. Fasting is feasting.

FASTING IS FEASTING

There's a passenger train that takes you from Oklahoma City, where I live, to Fort Worth, Texas. Since Fort Worth is a neighbor to Dallas, where a lot of my friends and ministry partners live, the train has become one of my favorite ways to get between our two cities. The train has a small café on board stocked with instant coffee and frozen sandwiches. Conversely, the Fort Worth train station is nestled in a trendy part of town crammed with great restaurants. The train gets in a little after noon, perfect for lunchtime. Though I typically get hungry on the four-hour trip, I don't usually eat on the train. It's not because the food is inedible or atrocious. It's because the meal waiting for me is so much better. I don't want to fill up on train snacks when there's a gourmet lunch waiting for me at the station.

We fast so that we don't fill up on train snacks. We fast to save room for the gourmet meal with God.

God is more satisfying than food. In many seasons of life, hearing from him is more necessary than eating our next meal. The comfort our souls most need is found not in a full belly but in God's love. God has what we most crave, but we often dull the sharp edges of that craving with lesser foods. We don't want to wait for the meal at the station, so we settle for snacks on the train.

Physical hunger points to a deeper satisfaction we all crave. Fasting heightens those hungers. Going without food makes us feel our hunger for prayer. Staying hungry makes us experience our longing for God's presence. Without fasting, we silence our deeper longings by satisfying our basic ones. Satiating our simple desire for food quiets the deeper hungers for soul satisfaction. Food, drink, and bodily comforts, though not bad, can be used to numb, cope, and drown out any feeling of need or desperation. Fasting makes us embody how truly hungry our souls are for God.

Jesus said, "Blessed are you who are hungry now, for you shall be satisfied" (Luke 6:21). There is a satisfaction that outstrips the satiation brought by food. When we hunger and thirst for Jesus, his kingdom, and his will, he promises the blessing of this deeper satisfaction (Matt. 5:6). Psalm 63 names this reality with some of the most poignant language the Bible offers on the subject. "O God, you are my God; earnestly I seek you; my soul thirsts for you; my flesh faints for you, as in a dry and weary land where there is no water" (v. 1). This is the cry of a person hungry for God. This is the deep, belly-aching need that fasting is uniquely equipped to address. A few verses later, after describing himself as a desert traveler near death from lack of food and water, the psalmist describes what it's like to finally be with God as his soul desires. "My soul will be satisfied as with fat and rich food, and my mouth will praise you with joyful lips, when I remember you upon my bed, and meditate on you in the watches of the night" (vv. 5–6). Meditating on God through the night satisfies this hungry psalmist as if he has eaten a rib eye steak.

God has satisfaction, comfort, and fullness on offer that food cannot replicate. We eat food because our bodies need it to live. We fast because food isn't the only thing we need to truly live. A fast is an embodied proclamation to our own hearts that we need to feast on the one our souls desperately need. We fast when we are hungry for God's presence, voice, comfort, direction, or power. We fast when we want to feast.

Biblical fasting is not practiced by itself. Fasting is accompanied by another activity. This is different from many of the other doors we've explored. When you pray, you pray. When you sing, you sing. When you take communion, you take communion. But if all you do in a fast is stop eating, you've missed its most crucial function.

Throughout the Bible, people fast and pray (Acts 13:3), fast and petition (Dan. 9:3), fast and worship (Acts 13:2), fast and commune (Ex. 34:28), fast and repent (Joel 2:12), fast and commit (Acts 14:23), fast and mourn (2 Sam. 1:12), fast and humble themselves (Isa. 58:5). Fasting accompanies and intensifies other activities.

Fasting cannot exist alone because it is primarily not about emptying but about filling. The point of a fast is not to empty yourself and lose weight as a pious show to God and the world that there is less of you now. The point of a fast is to be filled with what you are most hungry for.

When Jesus was tempted to end his fast by providing for himself instead of relying on God, he said, "Man shall not live by bread alone, but by every word that comes from the mouth of God" (Matt. 4:4). Jesus was accompanying his forty-day fast with a feast. He was proving to his own heart what would actually sustain him. So for forty days he consumed nothing but the word of God. He was fasting from something good so that he could feast on something better.

We don't fast to go without and prove our devotion to God. We fast to feast on God and enjoy his devotion to us. We fast from food to feast on what we crave most—God's love.

MART'S STORY

In 1998 a group of men and women challenged me to do something that was way over my head.

That night the Holy Spirit prompted me with two huge ideas regarding this challenge. Never before had he given me such large visions for the future. All I could do was to write them down in my journal. To say I was overwhelmed would be an understatement. So I prayed, "Lord, I'm going to fast one meal a day till you send someone to do what I was challenged to do."

I was desperate enough that fasting sounded like a good idea. Like someone who thinks tithing is the pinnacle of giving, I thought fasting one meal the next day was going to take me to the mountaintop! So far that year, God had been speaking deeply into my life, so I expected a quick answer. Every day, for those first few days, I expected a miracle. But one month went by, then two, three months, and four months later I was still fasting one meal a day and waiting on God.

I needed to take a business trip to Hong Kong and wasn't sure what to do. I didn't want to break the fast, but I also knew I would be served meals and snacks on my three upcoming flights. As I boarded the first plane, I said a quick prayer: "Lord, I'm not sure how to keep this one-meal-a-day fast, so I'm not going to eat until I get hungry." My plan was to take the twenty-four-hour trip to Asia, get some rest, and get up first thing the next morning and have a wonderful breakfast.

My first morning in Hong Kong, I went to a restaurant to have breakfast, but I wasn't hungry. I went to lunch that afternoon, but again I wasn't hungry. The same thing happened at dinner.

What's going on? I wondered. To my amazement it continued all week. I went to restaurants expecting to have an appetite, but I had no desire for food. Instead, I was eager to see how the Lord would speak to me halfway around the world.

On Wednesday evening I decided to attend a church service. After I walked through the front door and went up two flights of stairs that led to the auditorium, the first thing I saw was eight hundred Chinese men and women standing and praising the Lord. The singing was in Cantonese and I couldn't understand it, but still it touched me so deeply that I started to cry.

Once again, I prayed: "Lord, it's going to be difficult for me to hear from you, since I don't understand this language."

A guest speaker was introduced as a pastor from Indonesia who didn't speak Cantonese. Instead, he would be preaching in English with an interpreter. I thanked the Lord!

I listened with my notepad in hand, ready to write down anything the Lord would speak to my heart. I was in the midst of the longest fast I'd ever done and twice the pastor shared about people who fasted for forty days. "Lord, anything but that," I prayed.

When I arrived home, my wife hugged me and said, "You sure feel thin!" I told her I hadn't eaten since I'd left, more than seven days ago. At first, she was concerned about my health until I shared how the Lord was working in my life.

Back home, I went to many meals with my family intending to eat if I got hungry, but for forty days I never did. It was a miracle. Not only had God sustained me through four months of fasting one meal a day and then a forty-day fast, he also spoke to me and gave me vision and clarity for those two huge initiatives. He also gave me a defining phrase to help focus my life's purpose.

My forty-day fast ended on Thanksgiving Day, and I looked back through my Bible at all the verses the Lord used to minister to me. The theme I saw emerging was "less of me." It was funny because I had lost forty-seven pounds and got down to 130, so in a physical sense there was less of me. But spiritually, I noticed my desires for the things of this world were lessened as well. Through fasting, the Lord was teaching me that as I decreased, he would increase in my life.

For the past twenty-five years, fasting has been a regular part of my life. I fast because intimacy with God is our highest calling. Again and again I have found that God doesn't speak any louder when I fast, I just listen better.

FASTING IS FOR YOU

We don't fast because our bodies are bad. We don't deny ourselves food because eating is bad. We don't go hungry to whip ourselves into shape or punish our unruly flesh. Fasting is not a punishment for being human. Fasting is not against you, it is for you.

During Paul's ministry, a church in Colossae started to believe that they could earn or manufacture encounters with God through ascetic practices such as fasting. They would deprive themselves of good things and treat their bodies harshly. They did all of this to try to rid themselves of sinful desires and gain some mystical union with God (Col. 2:18–23).

In his letter to this struggling church, Paul tells them that treating their bodies so severely will not put their sin to death or satisfy their desire for communion with God. Instead, Paul tells them to feast. He tells them to set their minds on Jesus, what they have been given in him, and his return (3:1–4). The Colossians were using their fast to punish themselves and get God's attention. *If we beat the bad out of us,* they thought, *God's goodness can come in.* But fasting is meant not to punish you but to bless you.

Mart said it best. God doesn't speak any louder when we fast, we just listen better. God does not need you to fast for him to move. He is not waiting on you to fast before he releases a gift for you that he is stingily holding on to. God is always at the door knocking. A fast puts us in the thin place near the door where we can finally hear the knock and receive him as our guest.

Fasting does not grab God's attention, it grabs ours. Fasting is a powerful way to tell our forgetful souls what is truly satisfying. It brings us back to what we know is most important but so easily deprioritized. Hunger pangs, disrupted rhythms, and awkward social situations wake up our slumbering spirits and tell them it's time to eat. Fasting is not for God, it is for you.

We need fasting to train our palates for better cravings. Food is excellent. In my opinion, it is one of the greatest gifts God has given us to enjoy. As our palates mature to enjoy new spices, textures, and flavors, we learn to enjoy a wider array of dishes and appreciate them with growing complexity. But we also need to develop our spiritual palates. We need to train our desires to appreciate what tastes best, what satisfies the deepest. Fasting gives us the opportunity to explore new flavors in our hunger for God. We get to experience new ways he meets our needs and calms our cravings. Fasting teaches us how to hunger for the right things. We fast to eat the food that Jesus said he had but his disciples knew nothing about (John 4:32). We fast to feast on the best thing for us—God himself.

Are you hungry for a real meal? Then you're hungry for a fast.

TWELVE

SABBATH

The Sabbath was made for man,
not man for the Sabbath.

—MARK 2:27

> **Unlearn:** God loves me because of what I do.
>
> **Learn:** God loves me when I do nothing.

IT'S NOT UP TO YOU

When I was in college, I read a powerful Christian book that opened my eyes to Jesus' concern for the poor and his work alongside the marginalized. This book created a new ritual for me. Nearly every spare afternoon I had after class and every weekend, I went downtown and walked until I found someone in need whom God wanted to put across my path. After a while, I met others who were engaging this community and joined their mission. Soon I wanted to help people in even worse situations. So a friend of mine from college and I started an organization that gave free goats to needy families in the Philippines to help them reach economic sustainability. My wife and I even moved to the Philippines just months after getting married.

The problem was I wasn't doing any of this strictly because I loved people. I wasn't doing any of this solely in response to how God had loved me. Deep down, I was helping the poor because I knew Jesus loved the poor and I really wanted him to love me too.

In fact, my whole Christian life had been built on these assumptions. When I'm good, God is glad. When I'm bad, God is mad.

I believed God loved me because of what I did. I needed to learn that God loves me even when I do nothing. I needed to stop all my doing and experience God's unconditional love.

This is why, as for millions of others, the good news of the gospel completely changed my life. My heart learned what a seminary degree couldn't teach it. When Jesus said, "You did not choose me, but I chose you," he meant it. He really did choose me, he loves me, and he is pursuing me. When Jesus said, "It is finished," he meant it. His work on the cross finished all the work needed to reconcile me to God. When Jesus said, "Come to me, all who labor and are heavy laden, and I will give you rest," he meant it. I was exhausted from trying to earn his love. I was weary from trying to be good enough, effective enough. I was heavily laden with the burden of effort to be worth loving. But I could just come to Jesus and know that he loves me, has done the work for me, and now invites me into a different way of living. A way marked by rest.

Whether Jesus loves me isn't up to me. It's up to him. He just loves me. Whether Jesus loves you isn't up to you. It's up to him. He just loves you. You can't do more to earn this love or do less to lose it. So however weary you are and whatever is weighing you down, let's look at how we can live a life marked by the rest God created us for.

MADE FOR REST

The best way to be human is to be like God. We are made in God's image. When we do the kinds of things God does, we act consistently with our nature. We go with the grain of the universe. We match the fabric of reality. Conversely, when we act in ways that don't image God, we go against our design and our humanity breaks down.

We were created for good work. The story of the Bible begins with God working in creation. He puts Adam and Eve in the garden and gives them dominion to continue his work. We were made to work. Work is holy. When we work like God, we look like God.

But we were also created for rest. After six days of work in creation, God rested on the seventh (Gen. 2:1–3). He didn't rest because he was tired or lazy. He rested because rest is good. The word *sabbath* means to cease, to stop. At the very beginning of our whole story, God tells us it is good and godlike to stop and rest. When we rest like God, we become like God. We move with the grain of the universe and the fabric of reality. We sync up with why we were made. Conversely, when we refuse to rest as God did, we do damage to our design. Ceaseless work and sporadic rest make us less like God and less human.

Why would God rest and build a need for rest into our DNA? Because he loves us. When God inaugurated the first Sabbath day with his rest, he blessed the seventh day. God packed this day of rest with goodness, life, peace, and gifts. God stopped and enjoyed what he had made and invited his creation to do the same.

Rest was not the only distinct part of the seventh day. In the creation story, the day doesn't end like the other six days of work do. The other days of work, when God made the sky, sea, or animals, end with the same phrase: "There was evening and there was morning." After the day of work, the sun went down and the sun came up. The day was over and a new day started. The day of rest is different. Genesis never says that the sun sets on the day of rest. While the good work in the garden continued, all of it was meant to be marked and defined by the perpetual day of rest.

God completed the work on day seven. Out of that completed work, Adam and Eve would work. They would work in the garden, but the work was to be defined by rest. Adam and Eve's position in the garden wasn't up for review each time they poorly weeded a field. God's presence with them didn't withdraw if their harvest of figs that day was less than normal. God did not love them because of what they did. God loved them even when they did nothing. The seventh day, the Sabbath, proved that they could stop doing and still experience God's unconditional love.

The life God intended for us was one constantly illuminated by his light of completed work. That's the pattern. God finishes the work first and then invites us into it through his rest. Yes, we continue to work. In fact, God created us with specific good work planned for us to do (Eph. 2:10). But this work is not driven by the cruel taskmasters of guilt, insecurity, fear, and constant demand for more. Jesus leads us in the work we take on. That is a job that always begins with his "it is finished."

God does not love us because of what we do. He loved us and finished his work for us before we had done anything. God loves us even when we do nothing. Stopping in the Sabbath teaches us to experience God's unconditional love.

Whether it is our own salvation or the specific vocation he has us doing in the world, Jesus has already completed what we are walking out. This is the truth that allows us to stop and rest. We can cease from our work because we know God worked first. Our standing with God and our impact on this world are not dependent on us. They are dependent on God. It's our job to trust that this is true.

MART'S STORY

Throughout my life, my parents modeled giving 10 percent of their money to God, and often much more. It was easy for me to believe that 90 percent of my income with God is greater than 100 percent without him. What I was much slower to grasp is that six is greater than seven. Trusting God enough to sabbath one day a week was a bridge too far for me.

During the early days of Hobby Lobby, our stores were closed on Sundays. But as competition came into town, we feared losing out on sales, so we opened on Sunday afternoons. Those hours on Sundays became our best per-hour sales of any time in the week.

But after a few years, our family got convicted by the Lord that we needed to obey God's fourth commandment: "Remember the Sabbath day, to keep it holy. Six days you shall labor, and do all your work, but the seventh day is a Sabbath to the LORD your God. On it you shall not do any work, you, or your son, or your daughter, your male servant, or your female servant, or your livestock, or the sojourner who is within your gates. For in six days the LORD made heaven and earth, the sea, and all that is in them, and rested on the seventh day. Therefore the LORD blessed the Sabbath day and made it holy" (Ex. 20:8-11).

Our conviction was more like a dimmer switch than a light switch. The lights didn't come on all at once but grew slowly brighter. Even though we had a few hundred stores at this time, our faith was only big enough to close one store on Sundays. We started with our only store in Nebraska. Surely that wouldn't hurt the bottom line too much. Plus, we'd be able to watch how it affected our overall sales.

The newspaper caught wind of our effort and interviewed us about it. They asked whether we planned to close all our stores on Sundays. When we saw our answer printed in the paper a few days later, it was both embarrassing and convicting. We said, "If it works, we'll close all of our stores on Sundays."

If it works? Had we really based our obedience to God on its convenience for us? We were convicted that God commands us to obey him whether or not it works for us. He is our highest authority, not profit or convenience.

At that point we decided to close all our stores on Sundays. We did a few states at a time and, yes, it affected our sales negatively, but we felt good about obeying God's Word and, as a result, drew closer to the Lord as we depended on him to provide in other ways.

Even so, it was hard for me to adjust to not working at all on Sundays. I normally did at least some work seven days a week, so learning to rest stretched my faith. I had to fight to trust that Jesus can do more with me in six days a week than I can in seven.

I began to try to sabbath from dinnertime on Saturday to dinner on Sunday. I do my best to step away from my normal workload and instead set aside time to listen to God. I often take thirty minutes alone and start by praying, "Lord, if you have tried to speak to me this week and I didn't hear you, will you please speak to me again?" I then listen to the song "Speak to Me" by Kari Jobe and wait quietly, listening. Many times there are no earth-shattering revelations, but there have been a few times when I felt the Lord speaking to me.

One spring afternoon, I was outside enjoying the beautiful weather and listening for God's voice. Suddenly a strong wind blew through our back yard. At that moment I was reminded that the Holy Spirit can come like the wind. I sensed that afternoon that the Holy Spirit was going to show himself strongly on my behalf in the upcoming days. A month later at our illumiNations 2021 gathering for Bible translation, a prominent pastor used the phrase "Catch the wind" while preaching, and that weekend illumiNations doubled its best year ever, raising $84 million for the Bibleless.

I still have a lot to learn about Sabbath, but my next practice session begins again on Saturday night.

RISKY REST, ACTIVE DEPENDENCE

Rest lets God's love move toward you in a way that no other doorway can. This is not to say that there is anything wrong with the other practices we've explored. But the practice of meeting

God at most of the other doors involves some kind of action. Taking a Sabbath means to stop, to cease from all work. If you have a great experience of God's love through one of the other doorways, a small lie may present itself that you'll have to kill. The lie is that you earned some part of that encounter. Rest does the exact opposite. When we learn God's love for us while doing absolutely nothing, we experience his affection in one of its rawest forms. When we stop, we are completely dependent on the self-generating love of God. He loves us in our stillness simply because he loves us.

Rest is the active state of dependence. It's what absolute trust looks like lived out. Taking a Sabbath means taking a risk. You are risking your provision to rely solely on God's provision. The people of Israel experienced the risk of Sabbath after their rescue from Egypt. They were used to working as slaves seven days a week. They were used to a hand-to-mouth, daily-bread, eat-what-you-earn existence. God brought them into the wilderness and miraculously provided them with food. But there were two rules. First, they could take only what they needed for the day. No saving up for tomorrow was allowed. Second, they could not gather the miracle food on the Sabbath. Instead, the day before they could gather twice as much and prepare it to enjoy on their Sabbath day. This created real, day-by-day dependence on God.

The beauty of this story, and the beauty of Sabbath, is that God created us for dependence. It is the best way to be human. If we don't depend only on God, we can depend only on ourselves. If we don't depend on God, we have to carry the heavy load all on our own. The Sabbath is our reminder of how God created the world and how we are best suited to live within it. God did all the work to create the garden and invited Adam and Eve to enjoy it. While they joined God's work in tending the land, Eden was a dependent environment. We were created to depend on God.

There is no better place to learn God's love than a place of absolute dependence. When we know God's love does not depend at all on us, but only on God, we experience the unconditional affection of our creator.

God's love for us cannot be dependent on what we do when we are entirely dependent on him. But when we are entirely dependent on him, we know his love for us is not dependent on what we do.

The Sabbath is our weekly reminder of what work often leads us to forget. Six days a week of having people depend on us, solving problems, providing, and being essential can make us believe that we are what we earn. But once a week, when we stop all the work and give ourselves in utter dependence to God, the lies unwork themselves. On that day, we get to experience a love we did not deserve, a rest we did not earn, and a way of life we would not have invented for ourselves. The Sabbath reminds us that God loves us no matter what.

Can you stop? Can you rest? Can you receive the love of God that pursues you even when you do nothing to deserve it?

PART FOUR

LEARNING TO BE LOVED BY LIVING IT OUT

God loves you. He is walking through the thin places to get to you. Before you do anything to pursue him, he is already pursuing you. Give yourself a moment to know this truth, to believe it, to learn it. God's love changes your life. His love fills your life. His love is best experienced when lived out. Take a breath. Know you are loved. Breathe out. Continue when you're ready.

THIRTEEN

OBEDIENCE

If you keep my commandments, you will abide in my love, just as I have kept my Father's commandments and abide in his love.

—JOHN 15:10

Unlearn: I obey God to prove I'm good and worth loving.

Learn: I obey God to experience his goodness and love.

THE GRAIN OF THE UNIVERSE

I've always had a fascination with asking why rules exist. In elementary school I asked my teacher why gum wasn't allowed in class. "Because it's the rule," she replied. This isn't an answer—the rule exists because it's a rule. Even my third-grade brain knew that argument was circular. But I often heard the same thing when asking about the "rules" of the Bible I heard growing up. "Because God said so" was often employed as the Sunday-school teacher's question-ending trump card. In middle school I got a better answer. I asked a teacher why we had to have hall passes to go to the bathroom. "So the principal doesn't think you're skipping class," she said. That's an answer. The rule exists to keep me out of trouble. The rule is for my good.

For most of my Christian upbringing, answers in this vein were the norm. You don't have sex outside of marriage to avoid STDs, pregnancy out of wedlock, and the psychological baggage that comes with bringing experience with past partners into a marriage. The rule about sex was for my good.

While there is merit in answers like these, and I'm not attempting to discredit them, there is still a better answer for why God gave us commands to obey.

It's easy to believe that we obey God to prove we're good and worth loving. But in reality we obey God to experience his goodness and love. We need to see God's commands, not as restrictions to avoid or merits to earn, but as an adventure with God into his goodness and love.

God's commands reflect who he is. Intimacy between one husband and one wife tells us the story of God's faithful commitment to his one bride, the church. The prohibition of murder tells us that God values life's flourishing. The command against envy tells us God is content and desires us to have contentment in life as well. God's commands show us how to be like him. God is different, what the Bible calls *holy*. When we act like him, we are holy too. It's not a wonder that in the book of Leviticus, at the center of the Law, this truth is repeated again and again—"Be holy, for I am holy" (11:44, 45; 19:2; 20:26; 21:8).

Why should we follow God's laws or rules? It's not just because God said so or because it's for your own good, although both are true. We obey because obedience is the best way to embody and experience who God is and what he's doing in the world.

We don't obey to prove we're good and worth loving. We obey to experience God's goodness and love. God gives commands to show us who he is and teach us how to be like him. When we obey these commands, we also inhabit his character, including his love.

LOVE AS OBEDIENCE

Love and obedience are inescapably linked throughout the Bible. As Jesus himself taught us, "If you love me, you will keep my commandments" (John 14:15). This was not a new idea, but one repeated again and again at the beginning of the Bible. When the Israelites were about to enter the promised land, God told them that their love for him and their obedience of his commands were interlinked. Moses told the people to be "careful to keep all this commandment, which I command you today, by loving the LORD your God and by walking ever in his ways" (Deut. 19:9; see also 6:5; 7:9; 10:12; 11:1, 12; 30:16, 20).

To love God is to obey God. To obey God is to love God.

But before we fill in all the blanks of what this means, we need to take a step back and ask what commandment God wants us to obey. The answer is the same in both the Old Testament and New, on the lips of both Moses and Jesus.

If we do not answer this question the way the Bible teaches us, we are at risk of answering it ourselves. When we do this, we tend to fill in the blank of what obedience means with things such as perfection, achievement, and religiosity. When we hear that loving God means obeying his commands, we think that our love for God is measured by our sinlessness, righteousness, and holiness. The more we obey, the more we love God and are loved by God. The better we behave, the closer to God we get. Our perfection ramps up God's love for us, while our sins tone it down to a tepid trickle. This is untrue.

It is so important for us to get this right. What is obedience to God? Let's look at the book of 1 John in the New Testament to answer this question.

"This is his commandment, that we believe in the name of his Son Jesus Christ and love one another, just as he has commanded us. Whoever keeps his commandments abides in God, and God in him" (1 John 3:23–24).

When we think about obeying God, we tend to think about issues of morality—the shoulds and should nots of Scripture. We think about sexual purity and fiscal generosity. Or maybe we think about faith activities such as prayer, Bible study, church attendance, and service. All of these are good things that we will do as we follow Jesus. But they are not the primary focus of biblical obedience.

The number one command of God that we are to obey is to love him. That command gets sharpened with the coming of the Christ. We are to love Jesus and believe in him.

The primary work of obedience for the Christian is to love Jesus.

Jesus said as much the night he was betrayed. In one of his most famous illustrations, he calls himself the vine in a vineyard. We are the branches that bear fruit. But we bear fruit only if we abide in him. If we do not abide in him, we are cut off from the vine and thrown into the fire. So what does it mean to abide in him? Jesus tells us that abiding is keeping his commandments. Well, then, what commandments? Jesus answers, "As the Father has loved me, so have I loved you. Abide in my love. If you keep my commandments, you will abide in my love, just as I have kept my Father's commandments and abide in his love. . . . This is my commandment, that you love one another as I have loved you" (John 15:9–12).

Abiding in Jesus is abiding in his love. It is shaping your life, identity, and actions around the love Jesus has for you. That is his first commandment: "Abide in my love." The second commandment is similar. It is to love one another as Jesus has loved us. Those abiding in Jesus' love cannot help but extend that love to others.

Obeying God is loving God and loving others (Matt. 22:36–39).

God is not primarily after your actions. He is after your heart. He does not primarily want your behavior. He wants your affections. He does not primarily desire your moral perfection. He deeply desires you.

There are two reasons for this. First, God loves you and wants you to love him in return. There is a real relationship of burning love that God wants to enter into with you, and a real relationship means two people are in love. God already loves you. He also wants your love. Second, God wants to make you like himself.

Since he is the greatest being in existence, the best way he can love you is to make you like him. He deeply loves and so he wants you to deeply love. He knows that when you enter into the life-changing relationship of love with him, your actions will inevitably be changed to match his own.

But how do we "obey" the command to love God? How do we follow that rule? Do what John writes in 1 John—believe in Jesus. Jesus gave the same answer when speaking to a crowd who wanted to know what works of God they needed to be doing. "This is the work of God, that you believe in him whom he has sent" (John 6:29).

How is believing in Jesus obeying the command to love God? Because there is no better way to enflame our love for God than by putting all our trust in Jesus. In trying to obey the command to love God, we do not need to look to our own actions or efforts. We do not need to look at our own affections and hearts. We need to look to Jesus, his affection for us, his heart toward us, his actions on our behalf, and his efforts to get near us. As we look at the condescension of his incarnation, the forgiveness of sinners that marked his ministry, and the sacrifice of love he made on the cross, we will fall more and more madly in love with him.

That is why in the midst of Jesus' teaching about abiding in him he reminds us to focus not on our pursuit of him but on his pursuit of us. "You did not choose me, but I chose you and appointed you that you should go and bear fruit and that your fruit should abide" (John 15:16).

Learning to believe in Jesus is learning to receive the greatest love in existence. And as such a love grabs your heart, it will create the obedience God commands. You will not be able to restrain your love for God or others.

Our obedience doesn't prove we're good and worth loving. Our obedience is how we experience God's goodness and love. We join God's adventure to make us and our world more like him by obeying his commands.

MART'S STORY

In February 2021 I was having lunch with my dad when he asked, "How did the greatest love story of all time become known as a hate group?" He wondered aloud whether we could use media to help reshape people's misperception about Jesus.

"How would you go about running a national media campaign?" he asked. "How would you use media to raise up a beautiful Jesus?"

It was a powerful question, but I knew immediately that answering it was not my gifting. Plus, it wasn't my vision, it was his. So I prayed what Jesus commanded us to pray in Luke 10:2: "Lord, send me the right people. I need more workers for this harvest."

I reached out to a man I knew to organize the research and help find the right media company to partner with. Then I brought a few proposals to our wider family. What emerged was the "He Gets Us" media campaign. Our goal was simple: to rediscover the love story of Jesus.

I thought I was making the commercials for this campaign for other people, but one of my biggest surprises was how deeply I was touched. I remember when I first saw one of the commercials, the one called "The Physician." The images of hospitals and ventilators instantly took me back to when I lost one of my closest friends. I remembered the sadness and pain. Then the video ended with this simple line: "Jesus felt heartbreak too."

In that moment, intimacy with God happened for me. My obedience to what God had laid on my dad's heart unexpectedly drew me closer to my heavenly Father.

The commercials took off much faster than we thought. They received millions of views. In our monthly surveys, we found that many people who watched them made significant progress in coming closer to Jesus.

Samuel said it best in the Old Testament: "To obey is better than sacrifice" (1 Sam. 15:22). I have found this to be true. The simple act of obeying God's Word and God's Spirit is a pathway God uses to draw close to us.

THE ADVENTURE OF OBEDIENCE

When my wife and I were first married, we were living in a bad apartment, eating ramen, and trying to figure out how to pay the bills each month. She was a kindergarten teacher in Oklahoma, which was one of the lowest-paying states in the country for teachers. I had transitioned out of full-time employment to begin my poetry and teaching ministry. Suffice it to say, every invitation we got from a church or conference to speak meant we got a date night that month.

So when I got a job offer from a local up-and-coming player in the tech space, I was very interested. They wanted me to head up their marketing division, creating sales content and commercials for their emerging technology. The offer was compelling: a six-figure salary, equity in the company, and extra time off to focus on my poetry and teaching ministry. I was processing the offer with my dad when he gave me some really good advice. I had been invited to travel to England for a speaking tour put on by a small church network. My dad told me not to make a decision about the job until after getting back from England. Then, he assured me, I would know what God wanted me to do. All I had to do was obey.

The trip to England was phenomenal. My wife and I got to experience it together. During the day I would speak in high schools about our humanitarian work giving goats to poor families in the Philippines and our partnerships with groups such as TOMS Shoes. If the students asked me why we put so much of our focus on helping poor people on the other side of the world, I was allowed to give my real answer: We're living in obedience to Jesus. Jesus loved us and gave himself for us. Now we're loving our neighbors on the other side of the world, giving ourselves for them the best we know how. We saw English students baffled by the effect that Jesus' love can have on a person. It was a ton of fun. In the evenings I would speak at one of the churches in the network. The evenings were a one-hour mix of poetry and preaching revolving around the simple power of the gospel. Each night, we got to see avid church members reawaken to the beauty of Jesus and his good news.

After about ten days overseas, we headed back home. During a layover in the Minneapolis airport, I was sitting next to my wife waiting for our flight. Almost out of nowhere, with a striking level of clarity and conviction, I knew what God wanted me to do. I had to go all in on teaching people about Jesus. I couldn't give up 90 percent of my time to market a technology I didn't care about just because the pay was good. God wanted me to go on an adventure with him. I told my wife what I was hearing. She smiled and said, "I know." She was totally on board and on the same page.

I picked up my phone, called the business owner, and turned down the job. I laid my phone next to me with a sigh. *What have*

I just done? Have I doomed our family? Am I ready to live hand-to-mouth for years to come? I didn't have long to scrutinize my choice. My phone buzzed. It was an email from Mart Green. Yes, the same Mart Green who is writing this book with me. The email was simple. It said something like this: "Hey, David. God put you on my heart. Do you want to get lunch and talk about your financial needs?" Mart didn't know what was going on. But God did. And he was calling both of us on an adventure.

That email began a five-year partnership between Mart and Diana and me and Meagan that led to millions of gospel presentations made through online videos, an evangelistic curriculum for secondary schools in England, two published theology books, and a whole lot more.

That whole adventure came from two families obeying Jesus. Few moments in my life have made me feel more seen, more cared for, and more loved than when I got that email. When God's people obey him, the result is more of God's love in the world. And God is infinitely creative and compassionate in the varied ways he loves us.

Obeying God's will and words is not about earning his favor or staying out of trouble. Obedience is partnering with God to be on adventure with him in the world. It is tuning in to the ways God is pouring out his love to others and joining in.

God is calling you to obey him. By that he means he wants you to believe in Jesus, love him, and be on adventure with him. Do you want to go on this adventure with God?

FOURTEEN

GIVING

> Where your treasure is,
> there your heart will be also.
>
> —MATTHEW 6:21

Unlearn: I give resources away to earn more of God's love
and provision.
Learn: I give resources away to make more room in my heart
for God's love and provision.

UNREQUITED LOVE

Have you ever loved someone who didn't love you back? This is one of the most painful types of relationships to be in. This one-sided, unreciprocated relationship is called unrequited love. The unrequited lover builds their life around a person who is not fit or willing to love them back. Nevertheless, this lover bases their identity on this person, spends their time obsessing over them, and always wants more of them. The unrequited lover believes that this person will solve their problems, improve their life, bring them happiness, and provide them with satisfaction and meaning. But they never will.

If you have experienced unrequited love, you know the pain and disappointment that come with giving yourself to someone who will never give themselves to you. It breaks your heart, confuses your mind, and can ruin your life. Beyond the turmoil unrequited love puts you through, it also keeps you from giving your love to someone who can actually love you back. These broken places we put our love bring pain into our lives and keep us from learning that we are loved.

Despite the obvious pain it causes, Jesus taught that many of us willingly enter a relationship of unrequited love—the love of money (Matt. 6:24). Money is not wicked or evil, like some culprits of unrequited love, but it is a terrible place to try to receive love. Money is dead, inanimate, and unfeeling. It does not have the capability to love you back. Yet we often treat it like something we love. We build our lives around money, base our identities on money, spend our time obsessing over money, and always want more money. Money is what we trust to solve our problems, improve our lives, bring us happiness, and provide satisfaction and meaning. The problem should be obvious. Money can't do any of this because it cannot love us back.

Like all recipients of unrequited love, money can string us along, giving us just enough of what we need to keep us infatuated. But unlike most recipients of unrequited love, it's not money that is leading people on. It's not doing anything. It is lifeless. It's not sinisterly misleading us. Our hearts are. We give our love to an inanimate object. As with any unrequited love, this leaves us hurt and unable to receive the love we crave from another source.

This is one reason why Jesus told us that we cannot love both him and money. When we look to money to provide us with what we need most, we give it a role in our lives that only Jesus can fill. Money cannot love us. But Jesus loves us perfectly.

We need to make room in our hearts to receive God's love and provision. We do this by releasing our hearts from the love of money by giving it away. We generously give away money so we can make room to receive something far better.

Giving is such a crucial part of our relationship with God. This is not because God wants our money, wants us to have less money, or thinks money is evil. God wants us to give so we can rip our unrequited affections off money and give them to the one recipient of our love who can perfectly love us back. We cannot receive the fullness of God's love for us when we are trying to get what he's offering with money. God wants to solve our problems, improve our lives, be our provider, and give us satisfaction and meaning. God wants to show us the joy that comes from building our lives around him, basing our identities on him, spending our time obsessing over him, and always wanting more of him.

God wants you to give away money so he can give you something better—himself. Money is a fickle provider, but God is consistent. Money deceives your heart with its lies; God comforts your heart with his promises. Money gives you the crushing burden of self-dependence; God gives you the freedom and peace that come with dependence on him. God wants to replace your unrequited love with a never-ending love.

We don't give to earn God's love and provision. We give to make room in our hearts for God's love and provision. We generously give to make room to receive something better.

A GENEROUS LOVE

God is endlessly abundant. He does not have limits, account balances, or spending caps. But that is good news only if he is also endlessly generous. God has a limitless supply of resources, but how do we know he wants to give them to us?

God's generosity fills the story of Scripture. He created a vast universe that had done nothing to earn its creation. He gave eternal promises to a Babylonian pagan named Abram who did not deserve his covenant. He remained faithful to his people when they gave credit for their rescue from Egypt to a golden idol they made. He provided daily bread to grumbling and unthankful people for forty years in the wilderness. He gave opportunity after second chance after new beginning to the people of Israel even though they did everything to disqualify themselves from his generosity. The evidence of God's lavish generosity is staggering.

The ultimate proof that God is inherently and unendingly a God of giving is Jesus himself. God loved the world so much that he gave (John 3:16). Since God's abundance never lessens, what could God give that cost him something? What could he give that proved beyond doubt that he would not spare any gift to those he loves? God loved the world so much that he gave his only Son. As Jesus taught, whoever sees him has seen the Father (John 14:9). Jesus is the second person of the Trinity. He is not the Father, but he is nothing less than God himself. The God of no scarcity took on flesh and lived a scarce life. The God who cannot run out emptied himself to come to us (Phil. 2:7). The God who cannot lose anything lost his life on the cross. What proves that God is generous? He gave us himself.

Since God was willing to give us himself in Jesus, how can we argue that he would hold anything else back from us (Rom. 8:32)? God proved that endless generosity proceeds out of his inexhaustible abundance when Jesus gave up his life to save us. God is abundant. God is generous. Giving away our unrequited lover—money—teaches us to be loved and provided for by a boundless lover—Jesus.

God's generosity in Jesus proves that we do not give to earn more of his love and provision. God gave us the greatest gift of his love and provision in Jesus before we did anything to earn it. Instead, we just receive this gift freely. Now we give to make more room in our hearts to receive the love and provision God has lavished upon us in Jesus. We generously give so we have room to receive something better—Jesus himself.

MART'S STORY

My understanding of generosity began with my grandmother Marie Green. As a young person I heard stories of how she tithed on the gifts she received. She and Grandpa didn't have a lot. They were itinerant pastors, but if somebody gave her a coat or a gift of food, she would figure out how much it was worth and tithe on that.

These stories framed the foundation of my understanding of giving, but it was years later that the concrete was poured when I developed my own story of faith.

It began when I was thirty-seven years old. My wife and I sensed we needed to look for a new church. This was a big decision because our whole family and everybody I knew had been part of one denomination for my entire life. This included my grandparents, my aunts and uncles, and my parents.

So I was shocked when one Sunday night, my dad walked into the service of a new church we were visiting. How was it possible that out of all the hundreds of churches in Oklahoma City, my dad and I happened to visit the same church on the same night? Little did I know, God was up to something special.

A few weeks later, my dad and I were both visiting this church again, and they just happened to be promoting a ministry called OneHope. This ministry created a harmonized version of the four gospels for kids called *Book of Hope*. If you gave one dollar, they could print three of these and get them into the hands of children around the world.

I was moved to write down six numbers:

.5	2
1	2.5
1.5	3

After the service, I went up to my dad and said, "God gave me some numbers." As I shared them, my dad cut in and said, "Those are the exact numbers I got." I said, "Got for what?" He said, "Those are the numbers we should give every six months to support OneHope."

We knew God was challenging us to increase our family's giving, and those numbers were our stretch goals. We were going to start with the largest amount we had ever given in our lives, $500,000. Then six months later we would double that and give away a million dollars. Six months later, we'd give $1.5 million and keep that plan going.

It seemed like an impossible goal. The numbers just wouldn't work. We were going to try to outgive God.

Extravagant generosity is where the miracles happen. It's where we meet God and where he meets us. As we stretched to give, God showed us who he is again and again. Every six months we were able to meet our goal. It was unbelievable. Now it's twenty-six years later, our family still gives to OneHope, and we're ahead of our giving goals.

The Bible says, "God is able to make all grace abound to you, so that having all sufficiency in all things at all times, you may abound in every good work" (2 Cor. 9:8).

The story of the Bible and the story of my family have taught me that you can't outgive God. Our family mission statement is to "love God intimately, live extravagant generosity." We have seen that God is the greatest giver, and as we imitate him by giving, God loves to remind us who he is.

TREASURE IN HEAVEN

We do not give to earn more of God's love and provision. We give to make more room in our hearts for God's love and provision. We generously give to make room to receive something better.

Giving opens up our lives to learn the love of God. As we are generous with our resources, we both experience the greater generosity of God toward us and partner with God in his loving generosity toward the world.

Giving takes many forms. We can give our time, talent, and treasure. We can be generous toward others with our schedules and attention. We can show generosity by lending our unique gifts to those who need them. We can also give of our money, assets, and possessions. Beyond this we can be generous with our words, our thankfulness, our prayers, and nearly any other capacity God has put into our lives.

When we give, we position ourselves in a thin place to experience the love of God. We experience God's love through giving when we let go of trusting money to be our provider and give ourselves over to the good provision of God. God's love meets us when we relinquish possessions that have control over us. As they leave our grasp, we feel God swoop in and fill with fresh freedom the places where we used to be enslaved.

As Mart explained in his story about their family being stretched in generosity, you can't outgive God. You cannot, in obedience to Jesus, give something away that you won't get back with staggering dividends. That does not mean that God operates like a high-yield savings account with a fixed rate of return. God doesn't guarantee a 5.5 percent APY return on all charitable contributions. You don't put $10 in and get $10.55 back in a year. It does mean that God always rewards your trust in his abundance.

The reward, like the type of thing you give, can be nearly anything. God is endlessly creative in how he generously applies his abundance. New joy, peace, passion, purpose, provisions, friendships, or changed lives are but a sample of how God pours out his love upon us when we give.

It's important to note that we are not buying a reward that

God was conditionally holding back from us. Instead, we are putting ourselves into a position to receive what God always has on offer but our greed and fear cause us to miss.

The same idea is true about the eternal rewards Jesus talked about. Jesus promised his disciples that everyone who gives up home, family, and possessions for his name's sake "will receive a hundredfold" what they gave (Matt. 19:28–30). He promised this would happen "in the new world." This new world is what Revelation 21 describes when heaven comes to earth and all things are made new (v. 5). Jesus was talking about the end of time when God will dwell among us forever and bring perfection to a newly created heaven on earth. Jesus talked regularly about our generosity multiplying back to us in the new heavens and earth. He also taught about the pointlessness of storing up treasure on earth through stinginess and greed. Everything we enjoy here can be had for only a short and fleeting time. But what we will enjoy with Jesus will be eternal (Matt. 6:19–21).

Jesus wasn't talking about buying a bigger mansion in heaven by living in a smaller house now. He wasn't promising us that if we give away a Camry to a needy family on earth, we will drive a Ferrari in heaven. These things are not true treasure. Jesus was showing us how we can prepare our hearts to receive the kinds of unimaginable gifts that God's generosity has planned for us when we live together. Generosity weans us off the lesser, unsatisfying treasures that this world tries to blind us with. At the same time it prepares us for the surpassingly greater treasures of love, union, and peace we will experience forever with Jesus. Giving tunes our hearts for a better world.

Generosity not only prepares our hearts to enjoy the treasures of heaven to a greater degree but also sends real treasure ahead.

Again, I'm not talking about piles of cash. The treasures we can send ahead are the things that will have real value in heaven. The people our generosity reaches with the gospel will be our treasure in heaven. The beauty and justice our generosity creates will be our treasure in heaven. The stories, friendships, and goodness our giving makes possible will be what we treasure in heaven. When we set our hearts on stockpiling all our worth in those things, our treasure will no longer be what we own here but what we are creating there.

When you partner with the generous abundance of God now, you get to experience a little bit of heaven on earth now. Generosity pulls the sweetness of our future world into this present one. Valuing the things that Jesus says will last forever fills your life with the stuff of heaven instead of the stuff of earth. Don't fill your life with unrequited loves—possessions you give your love to that never give you love in return. Fill your life with what only generosity can buy. You will then learn how diverse and boundless God's generous love for you and the world really is.

We do not give to earn more of God's love and provision. We give to make more room in our hearts for God's love and provision. We generously give to make room to receive something better. God has endless generosity to pour out on you. Do you believe he is that generous? Do you believe he is that loving? If God generously gave his own Son, what will he not also give you in love?

FIFTEEN

FORGIVENESS

> For if you forgive others their trespasses, your
> heavenly Father will also forgive you, but if you
> do not forgive others their trespasses, neither will
> your Father forgive your trespasses.
>
> —MATTHEW 6:14-15

Unlearn: God forgives, but he doesn't forget. God has grace
but still holds a grudge.

Learn: God forgiving is God forgetting. God's grace cannot
hold a grudge.

A GRUDGE CANNOT LOVE

Before getting married, my wife and I got some great advice. Never keep score. Who did the dishes last? Who has put the kids down more? Who won the last argument? Who has messed up more recently? Whose turn is it to ask for forgiveness? Who forgave last? None of these questions are helpful because they are all keeping score.

You can also keep score in a relationship when you forgive but refuse to forget. You keep a record of wrongs and hold them against your partner. You say you forgive but still hold a grudge. Consider a wife saying "I forgive you" to her husband for forgetting a date night they had planned. But when the husband also forgets to grab milk on the way home, the wife reminds him of how he forgot their date. This happens all the time in relationships. We forgive, but we don't forget. We give a broken type of grace that still holds a grudge.

Keeping score is holding a grudge. It's saying, *You've done this one too many times. You always do this. This is just who you are.* We can be forgiven, but it's hard to feel forgiven if our mistakes keep being held over us.

The most important relationship in our lives is often held back by a grudge. When we think about God, we imagine a mind that remembers all our mistakes, carries the hurt of all our betrayals, and keeps record of all the times we've let him down. We believe God holds a grudge against us. It may be small. He may just be disappointed that we aren't living up to our full potential. Maybe his head just shakes slightly when he thinks about all the times we could have spent with him, shared our faith, or showed compassion to someone in need. Or the grudge we imagine God holding against us may be worse. Something in our past is so twisted and hurtful that every time God looks at us, he remembers it. We perceive that God is still holding on to a grudge.

We will receive God's love only in the same measure that we receive his forgiveness. If God is holding a grudge, God is holding back his love. When I hear words in the Bible that God uses to describe me such as "perfect," "blameless," "spotless," "clean," and "forgiven," I hedge my bets and shave the sharp edges off them. God can't call me perfect; he knows what I've done, what I think, and what I'll do tomorrow. He can't call me blameless when there is so much for me to be blamed for. God can't say I'm forgiven when I can't even forgive myself. I rob myself of the best news because I struggle to believe that when God says he forgives me, he means it.

I didn't know it, but in the back of my mind I thought God was holding a grudge against me. I thought God was keeping score. I thought my sins were still held over me.

This changed when I was on a solitude retreat. I spent the day reading Leviticus out loud. Yes, this is the book of the Bible with laws about how to sacrifice an animal. Yes, I did feel a little crazy reading it all out loud. Try saying "the long lobe of the liver" over and over and you'll see what I mean. But I knew God had some business to do with me regarding the forgiveness of my sins, so a whole book on atonement and sacrifices seemed fitting. I worked my way through the different offerings and what the priest was to do with each part of the animal.

After finishing Leviticus, I spent time in prayer asking God what he was saying to me through it all. He led me to the book of Hebrews in the New Testament, part of which unpacks how Jesus fulfilled the sacrificial system described in Leviticus. One line stood out. It said that the sacrifices prescribed in Leviticus "cannot perfect the conscience of the worshiper" (Heb. 9:9). Those who offered sacrifices were forgiven, but the sacrifice could not make their hearts feel forgiven. Their consciences still spoke against them. They felt as though someone still had a grudge against them.

This is how I felt. I believed in grace but still felt a grudge. I knew I was saved but struggled to feel loved.

God showed me that I knew I was forgiven through Jesus in my mind but that forgiveness had not made its way into my heart. My rational brain could repeat the truth that Jesus' sacrifice proved that God held no grudge against me. But my conscience still kept a record that I projected onto God. Legally, God acquitted me. But relationally, he still held a grudge.

I needed to experience the reality of God's forgiveness. It's not partial, halfhearted, or conditional. It is total, full-throated, and unequivocal. God's forgiveness is the kind that made the psalmist write, "As high as the heavens are above the earth, so great is his steadfast love toward those who fear him; as far as the east is from the west, so far does he remove our transgressions from us" (Ps. 103:11–12). On the cross, Jesus looked at the ones actively torturing, mocking, and killing him and said, "Father, forgive them" (Luke 23:34). His forgiveness is category breaking.

The only place where a lack of forgiveness exists between God and a Christian is in our own minds. We need to believe that God's forgiveness is total. He is not holding a grudge.

Where there is no grudge, there can be love. The sacrifices in Leviticus couldn't take away the sting of our condemning consciences. In the same way, the sacrifices of religion, good deeds, and new habits can't take away our condemning thoughts. But the blood of Jesus can make our hearts believe and know that God has completely forgiven us. For those in Jesus, he holds no grudge. He only loves.

I believed that I was forgiven, but I had not experienced it at this level. My imperfect conscience made me hold a grudge against myself. So I could not love myself. But when I experienced God's forgiveness the way he gives it—without a grudge—I could receive the titles he wanted to give me through Jesus. I am perfect, blameless, spotless, clean, and forgiven. This is not because I don't sin anymore or haven't messed up since. It's because this is how radically and totally God forgives.

If you hold a grudge, you cannot love. Love requires a giving of oneself and a treasuring of the other. Unforgiveness holds our hearts back and creates resentment. We can have well-wishes toward someone we haven't forgiven; we can even have a type of friendship with them. But there is an internal, and often external, leaning away and reservation. Any grudge starves out love.

MART'S STORY

My wife, Diana, was raised in a family where yelling and arguing were normal. When she was young, it seemed as though her parents were always fighting. She didn't even know what her parents' fights were about. She was just a child. To make matters worse, after an argument or anything upsetting, they swept it under the rug, never talked about it, and pretended nothing had happened.

In grade school, her mother came to her one evening and said, "Honey, your father and I are getting a divorce. You and I need to go into hiding because your father is dangerous."

This incident started the chaotic journey of her parents getting back together, breaking up again, and speaking terrible things about each other. At one point, her mom even disappeared for several weeks.

Diana was in shock and of course didn't have the tools to process any of this trauma. These hurts developed into anger and later bitterness. Into adulthood, Diana couldn't stand to be around her parents and didn't even want to talk to them. Her hurt was deep and she became very bitter.

Through a process of counseling and guidance, she understood what was causing her bitterness. God spoke to her, saying, "You have to forgive your parents." Diana knew she wouldn't be able to talk to them and discuss all the hurt. Her parents weren't the type to go to counseling together. She knew she needed to deal with it from her side. She knew she needed to forgive them, but it wasn't easy.

I spent eight years of my life making *End of the Spear*. On the fiftieth anniversary of the missionaries' deaths, we were onstage at Saddleback Church with Steve Saint, Mincaye, and the actual airplane the missionaries had used! We needed to be there with our friends for all six services that weekend.

In the first service, Diana heard the story of forgiveness preached. She thought, *Oh my goodness, I need to sit through six services on forgiveness.* During those services, Diana courageously decided to forgive her parents. She let go of the hurt and bitterness that had wrapped her up inside. Her bondage was broken.

The very next day, one of our kids had a basketball game, and when Diana arrived, she found that her parents were already sitting in the stands. Usually she would sit far away from them to avoid conversation, but this time she sat right behind them. God used her simple act of faith to begin healing her broken heart. Diana felt a new physical and spiritual freedom that carried over into her relationships. Her attitude toward her parents completely changed. For seventeen years, Diana was able to serve them with grace and patience as their health declined and eventually as her father passed away.

As her husband, I found it was so powerful to witness what God can do through forgiveness. He walked with Diana. He patiently led her to open her heart. He showed her what forgiveness looks like. Now I believe that when we choose forgiveness, God draws near.

FORGIVENESS HYPOCRITES

I used to be absolutely terrified to hold someone else's baby. Growing up as the youngest in my family, I somehow made it into adulthood without ever holding a newborn. How to cradle a tiny human never entered my mind until, as a young adult, all my friends started having kids. When visiting friends at the maternity ward, I would use my wife's giant love of holding babies as an excuse not to volunteer. She had younger sisters, was a babysitter, and volunteered in her church's nursery growing up. She had lots of experience; I had none.

When we had our first son, I was so anxious to hold him. I remember when the nurse took my flailing, weak, premature firstborn son and handed him to me for the first time. I was terrified. But as soon as he entered my arms, I knew I was his father and I knew how to keep him safe. Before long I was doing the one-arm "dad hold," where my son's head lay in my palm while his body dangled sleepily on my forearm. Within days, I was a pro.

Now, of course, I've held my babies for hundreds of hours. It became second nature. Experience changed me. My experience of holding my own baby has shaped me into someone who can happily and skillfully hold the fussy, hungry, or sleeping newborns handed to me by family and friends.

Forgiveness is experienced. When we experience God's

category-breaking forgiveness, it changes us. God's forgiveness makes us forgiving people. Though forgiving others may feel at first like an inexperienced young man being asked to hold a baby, the new life God gives us through the experience of his forgiveness shapes us into a people for whom forgiveness is second nature. Hand someone a baby and you'll know whether they've experienced parenthood. Hand someone an offense and you'll know whether they've experienced forgiveness.

Can you extend the kind of grace God has extended to you? Can you forgive as you've been forgiven? Can you give grace without holding a grudge?

In a long section of his most famous sermon, the Sermon on the Mount, Jesus teaches about hypocrisy. He points out people who give to the needy only to satisfy their own need for praise. He talks about people who honor God in public prayers to receive their own honor. He calls out people who fast to focus on God in a way that makes sure others focus on them (Matt. 6:1–18). Hypocrites are not people who try to do something and fail. Hypocrites are people who say they are doing one thing while doing the opposite.

The tragedy of hypocrisy is that it doesn't let us experience the good news of who we are pretending to be. Hypocritical giving does not give us the freedom and joy that accompany generosity. Hypocritical prayers do not give us the sweetness of God's presence in the quiet places. Hypocritical fasts do not give us God's far superior sustaining nourishment. Hypocrisy is a cruel way to be human. We do all the required actions of religion but experience none of the benefits of the relationship.

Jesus teaches that we can be forgiveness hypocrites too. We can claim that our worst sins have been forgiven by God, but we will not forgive the worst sins people commit against us. We warn ourselves of this tendency every time we pray the Lord's Prayer. "Forgive us our debts, as we also have forgiven our debtors" (Matt. 6:12). Jesus expounds on this request directly after teaching his disciples how to pray it. "If you forgive others their trespasses, your heavenly Father will also forgive you, but if you do not forgive others their trespasses, neither will your Father forgive your trespasses" (Matt. 6:14–15). Forgiveness hypocrisy is real.

If we refuse to offer forgiveness to others, we may be refusing God's offer of forgiveness to us. What we do when someone harms us, owes us, or injures us exposes what we believe God does when we do wrong to him. Our long memories and short fuses tell us what we think about God. We believe he is quickly offended and never forgets. After all, that's the way we are. When we refuse to forgive others, we are saying that we believe we have been refused. We are repeating the story of unforgiveness we have told ourselves. We've refused to experience God's category-breaking forgiveness, so others can't experience it through us. We can't forgive others, because we believe God has not really forgiven us.

Jesus is not saying that if you don't perfectly forgive you can't be perfectly forgiven. He is not saying that if you can't let go of every last grudge before you die, he'll forever hold a grudge against you. He is saying that experiencing God's forgiveness creates forgiveness in you. Your forgiveness isn't proving anything to God, but it's proving everything to you. God's forgiveness of our sins does not come from our forgiveness of others. Our forgiveness of others comes from God's forgiveness of us.

This is why one of the ways we experience God's forgiveness of us is in our forgiveness of others. When we forgive those who have deeply wounded us, we learn that God forgives us no matter how deeply we may wound him. When we forgive offenses we once thought impossible to forgive, we learn that there is no offense the love of God finds impossible to forgive.

There is nothing you can do to disqualify yourself from God's forgiveness. Do you believe that? Can you forgive like that? The more you do, the more you will learn God's grudgeless love for you.

SIXTEEN

THANKFULNESS

> Every good gift and every perfect gift is from
> above, coming down from the Father of lights,
> with whom there is no variation or shadow due
> to change.
>
> —JAMES 1:17

Unlearn: Everything I have I earned or deserve.

Learn: Everything I have is an unearned, undeserved gift
of love.

RECEIVE THE GIFT

Three months of sabbatical had led to this moment and I had no idea what to do with it. For nearly three months I had given days upon days of time to solitude with God. I had spent countless hours in prayer and absorbing his Word. I kind of viewed all of it as training for the capstone project at the end of my sabbatical: a week alone in the woods.

Months before my sabbatical began, I had booked a tiny home off the grid in the South Downs of England. My thinking was that I would need to force myself into an extended season of solitude since I probably wouldn't be disciplined enough to practice real solitude during my sabbatical. Surprisingly, though, I did. I spent days alone with God in a small farmhouse donated for my family's use during these sweet summer months. I got used to the slow, quiet rhythms of nothing to do but be with my Father. It became normal. I loved it.

So what was I supposed to do with this cabin of solitude? I didn't feel as though I needed to lock myself away anymore. Should I do something different? Should I skip it and stay home? Should I write this book? After my wife and I prayed, we felt that God was telling me to keep the cabin and go. But what God told me to do there caught me by surprise.

"Enjoy yourself," I felt him say. "Soak it up. Do what gives you life. Fill every moment of your trip with beauty, satisfaction, enjoyment, and bliss." So I ordered extra firewood, found the best farm-shop butchers to procure my steaks, and mapped out fifty miles' worth of hikes through the English countryside. I was giddy with excitement to revel in the gorgeous views, the delicious food, the joy of long walks, and the company of my God.

I arrived in England, rented a tiny stick-shift Fiat 500, and drove straight to a farm shop. I filled my basket with fresh butter, home-baked bread, and my favorite cuts of steak. Upon arrival at the cabin, I got a fire going outside and lit the coals on the small grill. My steak was seasoned and everything was ready for a picturesque night. But as I waited for the coals to heat up, I asked God, "What are you trying to say to me in this moment?" I started looking for a sign, straining for his voice, and feeling guilty that nothing was coming in such an idyllic setting.

Then, like a cool breeze, I heard these words: "Just receive the gift." I wasn't doing the one thing God took me out there to do. I wasn't enjoying the gift, I was ignoring it. I was using the gift as a means to another end. Surely God wanted to speak through the campfire, farmland, and perfect weather. I couldn't just receive it with thankfulness.

I felt as if I needed to earn or deserve everything I had. In reality, everything I had was an unearned, undeserved gift of love. I needed to receive God's gifts with thankfulness to more deeply experience his love.

As I asked God why it was so hard for me to just receive the gift, one answer came to the surface. I didn't believe I was loved enough to receive such lavishness.

I had to earn my place at that cabin. I needed a revelation that made it worth it, an insight that made me deserve it, a moment of repentance that changed my life so much that no one could dare judge me for going out there. I couldn't receive the gift because I didn't see it as one.

But as I confessed this, the world opened up to me in simple, profound beauty. The fire flames flicked with color and crackles. I thanked God. The steak on the grill sent up a pleasing aroma to my steak-loving nostrils. I thanked God. The green belt in front and the forest behind hemmed me into a secret paradise with no one but their maker. I thanked God.

As I did, I felt God's love with embarrassing force. Not only had he lavishly surrounded me with good things but he was inviting me to enjoy it all with no guilt and no shame, just thankfulness.

The beauty, provision, safety, comfort, opportunity, or simple pleasure right in front of us opens our hearts to hear some of the sweetest words we could ever hear from God—"I did this for you."

Thankfulness is enjoying whatever God has put in your life and recognizing where it came from. If we only recognize the source of the gift, we miss out on the enjoyment of it. If we only revel in the enjoyment of the gift, we miss out on the one who loved us so much that he gave it. Thankfulness invites us into the overflowing muchness of God. Sweet aromas, delicious food, colorful trees, laughing children, fresh air, green grass, a warm home, and a comfy sweater all spill out of God's creative generosity. He does not give us these things like a miserly Scrooge, crossing his arms to see how much we grovel with honor. He gives us these things for the same reason we give our kids toys on Christmas or sparklers on the Fourth of July. We want to see them smile. We want to feed their joy. We want them to experience the enjoyment of our affection for them and the splendor of life. Thankfulness opens us up to receive the gifts spilling out of God's loving heart.

But what happens when we don't feel thankful? What happens when the foundation of our thankfulness gets shaken by loss, suffering, and circumstances? We need a thankfulness that can't be shaken.

UNSHAKABLE THANKFULNESS

Paul talks about this unshakable thankfulness in his letter to a church planted by a friend of his. The letter is called Colossians. The church receiving Paul's letter is being spiritually shaken. False teachers and guilt-toting spiritualists have beset this baby church and are threatening to strip away their joy in Jesus. More than that, the city in which the church resides has been physically shaken by a massive earthquake that leveled many of its structures. So when Paul uses language like "shaking," you can bet his audience can relate.

When Paul offers this shaking church a source of unshakable thankfulness, it is no surprise that he points them to Jesus. After he warns them of the false teachers trying to delude them, he says, "Therefore, as you received Christ Jesus the Lord, so walk in him, rooted and built up in him and established in the faith, just as you were taught, abounding in thanksgiving" (Col. 2:6–7). Paul is offering these shaking Christians a way to rebuild their lives and faith and root them deeply so that they will not be shaken again.

The builder and the rooter is none other than Jesus. Paul does not say that they have received *things* from Jesus but that they have received Jesus himself. Paul even gives Jesus two humongous titles to overwhelm his readers.

Jesus is the "Christ." This is the same word as *messiah* from the Old Testament. It refers to the promised, anointed king whom God would send to right all wrongs and bring peace to his people. They have received a new king, a new leader, a new president, and a new world power. They have been given the ruler of the world.

Second, Paul calls Jesus "Lord." This is the title reserved for God alone. Jesus is God himself who has come to us in the flesh.

They have been given God. What a staggering statement. The gift that elicits unshakable thankfulness is the gift of God himself coming to be their forever king in the person of Jesus.

Enjoying the gift of Jesus undergirds our lives with a source of unshakable thankfulness. We are not talking about always being happy-clappy. Looking on the bright side is not thankfulness. Optimism is not resilient enough to endure the realities of living in this broken world. We need something deeper and steadfast. But when we are rooted and built up in the gift of Jesus, our Christ and Lord, we are unshakable.

Don't misunderstand Paul here. He is not talking about receiving the benefits of Jesus, what Jesus does for us. The benefits of Jesus are an important part of thankfulness, but the gift of Jesus himself is the priority. Just as I was looking past the gift of the cabin in the woods trying to find the deeper and more mystical meaning of it, we often look past the best gift of Jesus himself trying to find the other gifts he brings us.

Paul says that since we have received Jesus, the unshakable foundation of our thankfulness, we can walk in him. Jesus has given himself to us so fully and intimately that we can live with him step by step. He is our constant companion. Moment by moment, Jesus, the King of the world and God Almighty, is ever present, ever guiding, ever comforting, ever speaking, ever sanctifying, ever forgiving, and ever loving. Jesus never leaves us. Jesus never forsakes us. Jesus never stops loving us. Jesus never stops pursuing us. Jesus never stops healing us.

When walking a close friend through the worst trauma of their lives, I didn't know what to do. Should I bring them food, read the Bible to them, pray over them, clean their house? I didn't know. After several weeks of just being with them, not doing much, they told me the most amazing thing. "David," they said, "we are so thankful that you have just been here with us." That's it. The presence of a friend, the closeness of someone who cared, was all they needed to find thankfulness in a nearly thankless situation.

Jesus is the one who is always with us. He is the one we have been given and who walks with us every day. In Jesus, we can always be thankful. Thankful for his closeness. Thankful for his knowledge of us. Thankful for his empathy in every situation. The person of Jesus is present with us as a gift that cannot be taken away. We are his and he is ours. Jesus, and only Jesus, is the source of unshakable thankfulness.

MART'S STORY

I find it fascinating that God commands thankfulness. That tells me that thankfulness and gratitude are choices I can make by the power of the Holy Spirit. One thing I regularly thank God for are my friends.

Over the years, the Lord has blessed me significantly through friendships. One of those friends is Rob Hoskins. Rob is a man of generosity, humility, and integrity, and it has been such a gift to have him involved in almost all of the major initiatives I've been a part of.

In 2007 he called me and said that he thought I should meet a friend of his named Bobby Gruenewald. The wild thing was that Bobby lived in my hometown of Oklahoma City. When I first called Bobby, I heard about the big question he was asking: "Could we be at a moment in history when if we could just leverage the technology we have available today, it could transform how this generation engages with the Bible?"

Bobby's first step was to launch a new website where people could read Scripture on their computers and then tag their notes to a particular verse. The difficult part was getting the rights for the different Bible translations that he wanted on the website. Through my involvement with Bible translation, I had trusted relationships with many of the people Bobby needed to know. I was able to make introductions for Bobby, and within a year he and his team had the rights to the English Bibles they needed.

But the results of the website were not what Bobby had hoped for. The site had some traffic, but it didn't seem likely it was going to transform how a generation engages with Scripture. Right as they were beginning to shut the site down, Apple announced that they were making it possible to develop an app for the iPhone. What if we could build a Bible app that would be among the very first group of apps available in the App Store? Bobby wondered.

The team at Life.Church rallied to build a Bible app, and when Apple launched the iPhone, YouVersion was among the first two hundred free apps that were available in the App Store.

What if sixty thousand Bibles were downloaded in the first six months? we asked. That sounded good to us. The new iPhone came out on a Friday, and on Monday, Bobby called me. "Mart, you're not gonna believe this. We downloaded eighty-three thousand Bibles this weekend!" We were blown away.

Even more important than the number of people who installed it was the fact that we could see that people were using it. They were opening it on their iPhones and reading God's Word. It became apparent that God was doing something amazing and changing how people were engaging with the Bible.

After that first weekend, we kicked it into high gear and started strategizing. We knew we had to get ready for many more languages.

Now YouVersion has been installed by people in every country of the world. Current numbers show it is installed two times every second, twenty-four hours a day, 365 days a year. The total installs are more than seven hundred million and counting. In my opinion, it's the most effective tool of our time to help people come closer to Jesus.

I am incredibly grateful to partner with YouVersion and for my friendships with Rob and Bobby. God fills our lives with so many good gifts, and for that I am thankful.

FORGET NOT HIS BENEFITS

The gift of Jesus brings an unshakable thankfulness. Not only is his presence the present, but his presence brings presents. His nearness is the greatest benefit, but when he is near, he brings countless benefits.

Bringing the benefits of Jesus to mind swells our souls with thanksgiving. "Bless the LORD, O my soul, and all that is within me, bless his holy name! Bless the LORD, O my soul, and forget not all his benefits" (Ps. 103:1–2). One way we bless God is by thanking him for all he has done. Not only does this touch God's heart but it also heals ours. We can amplify our thankfulness by recounting all the good things Jesus has done for us. Consider this very small sampling.

- Jesus has loved us from before the foundation of the world (Eph. 1:4).
- Jesus, though God, became flesh to serve us (Phil. 2:6–8).
- Jesus heals our diseases now and will heal them forever (Rev. 21:4).
- Jesus forgives all our sins forever (Rom. 8:1).
- Jesus calls us his friends (John 15:15).

- Jesus died so we may have life (John 3:16).
- Jesus gives us resurrection life (Rom. 6:5).
- Jesus gives us his Spirit (John 14:25–26).
- Jesus gives us access to the Father (Heb. 4:16).

This list could go on infinitely. Jesus' benefits never end. Turning your mind to who Jesus is and what he has done for you is the best way to learn God's love through thankfulness. For as we receive gift upon gift, blessing upon blessing, with thankfulness we see how lavish God's love for us must be. Why would God do all of this for us? Why shower us with so much? Why pursue us so relentlessly? The only answer is that he loves us more deeply than we have the capacity to imagine. Thankfulness is the key to experiencing more of that unplumbable love.

We cannot earn or deserve the love and presence of Jesus. We cannot earn or deserve the presents of Jesus. Learning to be loved by Jesus teaches us how to receive gifts we did nothing to get. The more we enjoy and rejoice in the presence and presents of Jesus, the more we will learn to be thankful for every good gift around us. And the more we receive God's gifts with thankfulness, the more deeply we experience his love.

Can you receive a gift you didn't earn? Can you see how fully Jesus has poured out his love on you? This is where your thankfulness begins and where it always remains unshakable.

PART FIVE

LEARNING TO BE LOVED THROUGH GOD IN YOU

God loves you. He is walking through the thin places to get to you. Before you do anything to pursue him, he is already pursuing you. Give yourself a moment to know this truth, to believe it, to learn it. God lives in you. His power to love works through you. God wants to teach you his love in the most intimate way—by being with you. Take a breath. Know you are loved. Breathe out. Continue when you're ready.

SEVENTEEN

SPIRIT

If anyone loves me, he will keep my word, and my
Father will love him, and we will come to him and
make our home with him.

—JOHN 14:23

Unlearn: The Spirit is the power of God within us.
Learn: The Spirit is the person of God within us.

INTIMACY AND PROXIMITY

Long-distance relationships are hard. When my wife and I were dating in college, I knew I wanted to propose. The last summer before our senior year was coming up and we would be spending it apart. She would be traveling the country singing in a touring band that did recruitment for our university, and I would be interning at a church in California. I wasn't exactly worried about our relationship, but I knew what they say about long-distance relationships. There is something about intimacy that is unavoidably linked to proximity. Being close and being in love just go together. So before we parted ways for the summer, I surprised her with a proposal. When I put that ring on her finger, it was a promise that we would come back together for forever.

We need proximity with God if we are going to have intimacy. Yet that proximity often feels threatened. It feels like a long-distance relationship. I can often resonate with how the disciples felt when Jesus told them he was leaving them. Jesus said they were afraid with troubled hearts (John 14:27). It's no wonder. Jesus said he was going back to the Father, meaning he was going back to heaven. It doesn't get any more long-distance than that. This distance can feel like absence. I have written an entire book about the lived experience of feeling far from God (*When God Isn't There*). Suffice it to say here, this distance, whether real or imagined, makes intimacy hard.

The need for nearness to God is so incredibly important that the whole story of the Bible plays out its drama. We began in a garden with God, so close that we thought hiding in a bush would keep him from seeing us. When Adam and Eve ate the fruit, death entered the world, and the Bible equates it with being cut off from the presence of God. Outside Eden, the biblical narrative traces humanity's exile farther and farther east from God's presence. After God rescued his people from Egypt, he gave them plans for how to build a tent where they could be near each other again. But only the high priest, once a year, could enter into God's presence in this new mini Eden, called the Holy of Holies. The tent turned into a permanent temple, but even that was eventually destroyed— sending his people once again into exile and separation. The Bible tells the story of a long-distance relationship.

Then, across the distance, Jesus came to us. His coming is described as a new garden, tent, and temple being set up among us (John 1:14). God was healing the distance. Jesus said, "When you see me, you have seen the Father." God was breaking out of the Holy of Holies. We couldn't get back to Eden or enter into heaven, but Eden and heaven were coming to us. Jesus brought proximity and offered intimacy.

It's no wonder, then, that the disciples were afraid and troubled in heart when Jesus said he was going back to the Father. It seemed as if God was going back to Eden, leaving us in the east. God was going back into the Holy of Holies, leaving us outside. But this is not all Jesus said.

Jesus said that his leaving his disciples would be good for them. Jesus promised that when he went to the Father, he would send the Holy Spirit. "Now I am going to him who sent me. . . . Because I have said these things to you, sorrow has filled your heart. Nevertheless, I tell you the truth: it is to your advantage that I go away, for if I do not go away, the Helper will not come to you. But if I go, I will send him to you" (John 16:5–7). How could distance from the incarnate Son of God be good? How could introducing distance into a relationship that craves proximity be advantageous?

It's because Jesus' departure meant God would move closer than ever in the Holy Spirit.

Many Christians think of the Holy Spirit as an impersonal force rather than a personal presence. But the Holy Spirit is not just the power of God, it is the person of God. Through a relationship with the Holy Spirit, you can experience proximity to and intimacy with God.

TENT OF MEETING

Moses had one of the most unique and staggering ways to be close to God. He would pitch a tent outside the rest of Israel's camp while they were in the wilderness (Ex. 33:7). Inside that tent he would meet with God and talk with him face to face, as someone talks with a friend (v. 11). This was a real encounter with the glory of God. Moses' face would shine with the brightness of God's glory he saw in that tent (34:34–35). This proximity led to deep intimacy. So much so that the closing words of the books of Moses, called the Torah, say, "There has not arisen a prophet since in Israel like Moses, whom the LORD knew face to face" (Deut. 34:10). Face-to-face proximity created unmatched intimacy.

For the rest of Israel's history, this proximity with God's glory was limited to the Holy of Holies. Face-to-face intimacy like Moses enjoyed was not possible (Ex. 33:20).

Then Jesus changed everything.

While talking to his heartbroken and fearful disciples about why it was to their benefit that he should go away, Jesus explained the cataclysmic shift in proximity that the coming of the Holy Spirit would bring. Jesus said the Holy Spirit would dwell with them and be in them (John 14:17). God was not leaving, he was moving into another tent. But this time it would be the tent of our own bodies. No longer would people have to travel to a tent or building only to be kept out by walls and curtains that shielded them from the face-to-face presence of God. Instead, God would travel into the tent of our bodies, where we can turn to him and have an even more intimate proximity than Moses had (2 Cor. 3:7–18).

God's movement out of the Holy of Holies and into the hearts of his people was demonstrated powerfully when Jesus died on the cross. At the moment of Jesus' death, the curtain that separated humanity from the presence of God in the temple was miraculously torn in two (Matt. 27:51). The story of separation told from the beginning of the Bible was finally reaching its climactic resolution.

God lives within us. The New Testament goes so far as to call our bodies God's temple (1 Cor. 3:16). This indwelling is even deeper than proximity. The Holy Spirit in us creates a oneness and a union, as there is when a husband and wife are joined together in intimacy (Eph. 5:31–32). We have been given access to the intimacy with God we crave because of the proximity we have through the Holy Spirit.

The Spirit is not the essence of God, a part of God, or a single characteristic of God, such as his power or voice. The Spirit is the person of God living within you. You can build a relationship with God the Spirit. You can experience proximity and intimacy with God.

MART'S STORY

The Holy Spirit leads us in astounding and often unexpected ways. As we learn to pay attention to the Holy Spirit, who lives within us, we're drawn close to God and invited to join him in the ways he's bringing his kingdom on earth as it is in heaven.

In the spring of 2021, I began watching episode 1 of a TV show about the life of Jesus called *The Chosen*. I had sold *The Chosen* DVDs at our Mardel stores, but I had yet to watch it when a good friend highly recommended it and gave me a copy of season 1. In the final scene of episode 1, Jesus quotes Isaiah 43:1 to Mary: "Fear not, for I have redeemed you; I have called you by name, you are mine."

Watching this, I wept and wept and felt the Holy Spirit prompt me: "You are going to help serve the godly vision inside the creators of this show, Dallas and Amanda Jenkins." I wasn't sure how or when, but I knew I wanted to help.

Soon after, I shared with a group of friends that we ought to reach out to *The Chosen* to help them translate the show into other languages. I told them I did not have a connection to Dallas but would work on that. Six hours later, I noticed I had one of those little red dot notifications on my phone, and I don't like having those, so I checked my Facebook Messenger app, which I rarely do, to clear that red dot. Waiting there for me was a message from Dallas Jenkins.

One month later I attended the National Religious Broadcasters convention, where Dallas and Amanda Jenkins were screening episode 6 of season 2. Right before they showed the episode, Amanda shared a powerful story she'd heard years ago. A missionary team was working in a closed country where Bibles were illegal, and so they would go out under the cover of darkness to deliver Bibles. At one point their steering wheel jammed and their car veered right and came to a stop under a streetlight. There a solitary man was standing. Waiting. The man came up to them and said in broken English, "You have Bible. God told me to leave my village and come here. You have Bible." They gave him all the Bibles they had. The man paid them all of the money his village had collected, then began walking away. The missionaries called out, "Sir, we'll come, we'll preach. Can we come and minister to your village?" Over his shoulder he replied, "No. Bible preach!" And he walked off into the darkness. Amanda then concluded, "I love this show, but who cares? It's just a show. Bible preach." I really appreciated her perspective and humility.

After the episode, I met Dallas and asked him, "What's your goal for *The Chosen*?" He responded, "That one billion people would experience an authentic Jesus." Wow. I knew I could invest my time, talent, treasure, and trust in Dallas and Amanda.

A few weeks later our family agreed to start contributing financially to support translation efforts. I suggested we set up a nonprofit organization alongside *The Chosen* and also reached out to a friend of mine to see if he would be the CEO. Six months later this new nonprofit was set up, called the Come and See. *The Chosen* has reached into prisons and across borders in languages all over the world. People are giving their lives to Jesus and coming back to him in astounding ways. *The Chosen* has propelled people back into reading their Bibles to see Jesus for themselves. So far the episodes have been viewed more than half a billion times, with much more to come.

What an adventure I would have missed if it weren't for the Spirit of God leading and prompting me.

THE PERSON OF THE HOLY SPIRIT

During our summer apart, after the proposal, my wife and I did not see each other in person. I did not have her with me. I had her voice, because we talked on the phone. I had her thoughts and she had mine, because we kept each other in mind. I had her love, because we were betrothed. But I did not have her. I had parts of her with me but not her whole self. You could say I had her in spirit but not in person. Tragically, this is how many Christians think of the Holy Spirit.

The Holy Spirit is not part of God but God himself. He is not God's voice, promptings, or power, as if those aspects of God traveled from his presence to us through his spirit. That would make the Holy Spirit a *what*. When we speak of the Holy Spirit, we speak of a person, a *who*. God is not with us in spirit. God is with us in the person of the Spirit. The God of the universe is with us. That is why Jesus could say to his worried and fearful disciples that when the Holy Spirit came, "we will come to [you] and make our home with [you]" (John 14:23). Jesus was talking about himself and the Father. If the Holy Spirit lives in us and that means that Jesus and the Father do, too, it is because the Holy Spirit is God himself. This is the baffling mystery we call the Trinity—three persons, one God.

The Holy Spirit who lives within all Christians is God himself. Like God, and all persons, the Holy Spirit has emotions (Eph. 4:30). He has plans and desires (1 Cor. 12:11). The Spirit teaches (1 Cor. 2:13). He bears personal titles such as Comforter and Counselor. The Spirit leads (Rom. 8:14), compels (Acts 20:22), comforts (John 16:7), commands (Acts 8:29), and speaks (Acts 13:2). When we say that the Spirit lives in us, we are saying that the same God who created the universe, appeared to Moses, and revealed himself in Jesus is the same God who has made us his home.

Not only is the truth that God himself lives within us the most staggering truth to fathom, it is also one of the largest doors through which God has ever pursued humanity. He wants to move in with you. He wants to spend every second with you. God loves you so much that he wants to be one with you. If you want to learn God's love, you have all the nearness you need. Not his voice alone, guidance alone, or power alone, but God alone is in you. You have the most radical proximity required to pursue the deepest intimacy imaginable.

LIFE IN THE SPIRIT

The whole Christian life is about learning to live with the Spirit. The Bible calls this walking by the Spirit (Gal. 5:16), being led by the Spirit (Rom. 8:14), and being filled with the Spirit (Acts 4:8). In a sense, this whole book has been a reflection on how to live life in the Spirit. Life in proximity with God is marked by receiving his love and letting it change your life. Perhaps the greatest school of God's love is communion with him as the Spirit dwells inside you.

One of the biggest aha moments I've ever had came from reflecting on this truth. Often when I pray, I picture my prayers rising up. They travel up to God in heaven. This mental picture reemphasizes the long-distance relationship I often feel. But one day I realized I can talk to God as though he's right next to me— because he is. He lives within me. We are his temple.

Every Christian is like Moses going into the tent of meeting. We can commune with God right here in the tents of our bodies. The Spirit is with us. He talks to us, guides us, and comforts us. Life in the Spirit is a life lived in constant communion with God. Life in the Spirit is a no-distance relationship.

I invite you to build your relationship with the Spirit. You can pray to the third person of the Trinity. You can speak to the Spirit. Direct some of your prayers to God as he dwells within you. Ask him to speak to you. Ask the Spirit to direct you throughout your day. Process things with the Spirit. Consult the Spirit. Ask the Spirit for power, aid, and comfort.

God lives in Christians. This is one of the most staggering acts of love our universe has ever seen. Lean in to the beauty and mystery of this proximity. Practice communing with the Spirit and you will experience God's love closer than you ever thought possible.

EIGHTEEN

MIRACLES

If it is by the Spirit of God that I cast out demons,
then the kingdom of God has come upon you.

—MATTHEW 12:28

> **Unlearn:** God is uninvolved in our world.
> **Learn:** God involves himself in our world—sometimes through miracles.

AN UN-MIRACULOUS FAITH

My first mission trip was to Acuña, Mexico. As a junior in high school whose life had been recently transformed by the gospel, I was excited and extremely nervous. Each day we would go to villages where people lived in extreme poverty to see how we could help. Sometimes that meant providing a large bag of rice to feed a family or a new piece of sheet metal to patch a rusted hole in a roof. A few times we were asked to pray for healing. I had never done that before. The church I grew up in didn't practice the kind of laying on of hands and prayers for healing you see in the ministry of Jesus and his disciples. They didn't teach against it, we just didn't do it.

But in one dark home, we were introduced to an *abuela* who could not walk because of a swollen and bulging ankle. Something severe had to be going on because the ankle was purple, black, and red. It was so swollen that my fingers didn't touch when I wrapped my hands around it to pray. Not knowing what to do, I prayed. I asked for healing. After just a few minutes of prayer, the ankle began to shrink in my hands. The discoloration disappeared. My fingers touched. The ankle looked normal. The *abuela*'s face changed. She smiled with tears in her eyes and stood up in front of us all. She walked around the house, praising God.

The next day, as we walked around the village, a young woman who had heard the stories of what God was doing in their village through our group asked me to share the name we were healing and helping in. I had a translator with me and began sharing the gospel of Jesus with her through the translator. As her excitement and interest grew, I answered her questions before the translator spoke. Likewise, she could understand me without the translator. We were each talking in our own languages but understood each other perfectly without a translator. She was struck by the love of Jesus and we prayed together as she put her trust in him.

When I came home, I couldn't wait to tell my girlfriend (who is now my wife) what I saw God do. But when I told her, she said, "That didn't happen." She was raised in a Christian tradition that did not practice praying for miracles, like the ones I did, and taught that miracles didn't happen anymore. As I learned more about her tradition and met her pastors, I became convinced that I had made it all up. Maybe God doesn't do this kind of thing anymore. If he did, wouldn't we see it more often? Wouldn't Christians be aligned in their belief that such a world-changing power is in operation? My faith in the ongoing existence of miracles and my trust in what I had experienced disappeard for years.

I came to believe that God was basically uninvolved with the physical world. He was not personally engaged in altering the things I see, touch, and experience. But I needed to learn that God does physically involve himself in our world through miracles. God shows his love for our broken world by setting things right through the miraculous. We can learn to trust and experience God's love for us by asking him to do miracles.

Through countless miraculous experiences in my own city and abroad, my belief in God's continued supernatural activity has recovered. Even apart from my experience and the experiences of millions of others, the Bible itself has been the greatest source of my belief in and expectancy for miracles.

MIRACULOUS LOVE

What are miracles and why do they happen? Miracles are God's supernatural intervention in the affairs of the world.

But why would God want to intervene? What is his intention when he performs a miracle? While the individual circumstances surrounding miraculous events vary as widely as God's intention in each of them, we can safely say that God does the miraculous because he loves us and wants us to love him.

I took a week of solitude in a tiny cabin in the woods. My wife asked what I was most looking forward to, and I said, "Sitting under the stars." I wanted to get away from the light pollution of the city to see the black sky covered with starlight and planets. There was one problem: it was the rainy season. The sky was shrouded by clouds. On the first night, I couldn't see a single star. The forecast for the rest of my time there was identical. Overcast, cloudy, and a 100 percent chance that I would not have the clear, star-filled sky I hoped for. So I asked God for a miracle. I asked God for one night of stars.

A cloudy three days passed. There were no stars to be found.

On my second-to-last night before leaving, I sat at my campfire in prayer. I felt the Holy Spirit challenging me. A few months back, using the book of Genesis, he broke through my defenses and excuses to convince my heart that I was truly chosen and loved by him. The Spirit led me to Genesis once again and the story of Abraham. God chose him and promised him that his offspring would be as numerous as the stars in the sky. I felt the Holy Spirit leading me to look up. Through the trees I could see tiny dots of light. It had been cloudy all day. I ran from the campfire and out into an open patch of grass. The whole sky was clear. Stars without number filled my eyes. Laughing with joy, I felt God say to me, "I did this *for you*." God miraculously worked through weather patterns and synced them up with his message to me just so my heart could feel his choosing and love.

God physically involved himself in my world to show me his love. When I asked God for a night of stars, I was trusting that he loved me enough to do it. Whether it happened or not, I voiced my trust that God's strength and affection were powerful enough to make this happen. God showed his love for me through a miracle.

There is a strong connection between love and miracles. Throughout the Bible miracles fuel the worship of, trust in, and love for God. After God parted the Red Sea, rescuing Israel from Egypt, Moses and the people sang a song to God proclaiming his power and glory (Ex. 15:1–21). "You have led in your steadfast love the people whom you have redeemed; you have guided them by your strength to your holy abode" (v. 13). God miraculously kept Israel alive in the wilderness for forty years with a supernatural supply of food and travel gear that never wore out. God said that, in these miracles, he carried Israel like a father carries his son so that his people would learn to trust him (Deut. 1:31–32). After so many of Jesus' miracles, the people he rescued worshiped him, shouted for joy, and went away loving him. God performs miracles to move our hearts toward him in love.

Outside the resurrection, the greatest miracle our world has ever seen is the incarnation of Jesus—God dwelling with us in the flesh. There has been no greater supernatural intervention in the affairs of the world. The God of all creation became created. The inventor of worlds and wombs became a fetus. The Father of all life was born as a human. When we look for a reason for such a benevolent miracle, there is only one answer. God loved the world so much that he gave his only Son (John 3:16). The miraculous is a result of love. God performs miracles because he loves us.

For centuries the Hebrew people placed their trust in God by praying for him to visit them. They asked for the Messiah to come. They were trusting and experiencing God's love for them by asking him to perform a miracle. And God was pleased to answer this prayer because he loves us.

MART'S STORY

In 1998 I had a prompting of the Holy Spirit, something I felt the Lord put on my heart that was going to happen in the future. It was going to be a project so big that no ministry could do it alone. And it was also so big no gospel patron could do it alone. I knew it would take a miracle. What I didn't know was that, twelve years later, God was going to fulfill this dream by aligning my path with that of an NFL kicker named Todd Peterson.

Todd's years of success in professional football gave him influence and relationships with many athletes and artists. One of his college teammates had become a Bible translator, and that opened Todd's eyes to the needs of billions of people around the world who didn't have God's Word. Todd wanted to use his platform as a football player for God's glory, and God gave him a vision to convene influencers around the cause of Bible translation.

When I first met Todd, a few of us—under the name of Every Tribe, Every Nation—had already been working on a digital Bible library, a place where all the Bible translations in all the languages in all the world could be easily accessed. Our hope was to unite Bible-translation agencies to share the digital versions of their translations.

Todd joined the small group of us with Every Tribe, Every Nation and we began meeting every month with the CEOs of a few Bible-translation agencies. We'd fly into the Dallas–Fort Worth airport and meet to build trust and further collaboration. Never before in history had these agencies worked in unison for a common goal. Instead, each organization labored in its own silo, seeing part of the puzzle but not having a picture of the whole thing. We wanted to work from one plan with no duplication of effort so that Bible translation could be done better, faster, and cheaper, because we believe everybody deserves to have God's Word in the language they know best.

Around that time, Todd hosted a big event in partnership with an organization called the Seed Company to celebrate the completion of the one thousandth Scripture translation. It was a one-time gathering called illumiNations, and I was struck by the excellence in execution and the stunning generosity I witnessed there. To my amazement, the people at that event committed a record $21 million for Bible translation. A few months before, I had tried a similar event to raise funding collaboratively with Every Tribe, Every Nation that raised zero dollars. Nothing! Feeling as though I was in a dark room with no way out, I canceled our next event. It was a time of mixed emotions. I was thrilled for what had just happened at illumiNations, but I couldn't see the way forward for what I was asked to lead.

A few weeks later, Todd called to talk about illumiNations being an ongoing gathering. He suggested this gathering be the main event for several Bible-translation agencies, not just one. I would barely let myself dream about this because I thought there was no way the Seed Company board would approve sharing their highly successful fundraising gathering with other agencies. But I also wondered whether this was my original vision of a project so big that no ministry could do it alone.

The next time I talked to Todd, he brought it up again, and I asked,

"What did the board say?" He replied, "They didn't say yes, but they didn't say no."

At that point, I felt permission to start dreaming of a miracle. Out of the generosity of a handful of leaders, an incredible movement of patrons called illumiNations was born. Over the past ten years, eleven Bible-translation agencies have come together in an unprecedented way to raise funding to eradicate Bible poverty. Together, we are pursuing the same all-access goals: By the year 2033, 95 percent of the world will have a full Bible, 99.96 percent will have at least a New Testament, and 100 percent will have at least the first twenty-five chapters. Also, the top hundred languages in the world will have at least two current translations. What we thought would take 150 years under the old translation model could now be possible in our lifetimes.

So far, more than $430 million has been committed for Bible translation, and the speed of translation has increased rapidly. It's going to take even more miracles to complete our goals, but we believe God can do it, and when he does, we will be the most Scripture-engaged generation in history.

The miracle of seeing these leaders, organizations, and patrons work together has deepened my intimacy with God, strengthened my faith, and brought into my life one of the best gifts God gives: trusted relationships. Looking back to 1998, I see now that God hinted at what he was about to do so that I would know it was his doing, that it was his miracle for his glory.

WHY JESUS PERFORMED MIRACLES

Have you ever wondered why Jesus performed miracles? Why did he heal the sick, cast out demons, multiply food, and raise the dead?

There are several reasons. Jesus was demonstrating his identity as the Spirit-filled Son of God. Jesus was giving his world signs and wonders to call them to belief. But Jesus also performed miracles because he loves the world and wants to heal it.

When Jesus' friend Lazarus died, Jesus wept (John 11:35). He was moved by his hatred of death and his love for the world he made to receive life. When he raised Lazarus from the dead, Jesus was fixing a broken part of his world. Jesus was setting things to rights.

God made the world to be his kingdom. It was to be an Eden-like place where life flourished. It was to be a place where he lived with his people and everything was fruitful and multiplying.

Jesus performed miracles because he wanted to bring God's kingdom to earth. He wanted to push back the sin, darkness, brokenness, and death that had taken over.

Jesus cast out demons because humans are meant to be God's dwelling, not the demons'. Jesus healed the sick because in his kingdom there will be no illness. Jesus raised the dead because when he comes as King of the earth, death will be no more.

Miracles are God's way of bringing heaven to earth.

God performs miracles because he wants us to experience his kingdom here and now. He wants us to know his love, protection, and care. He wants us to trust that he is making all things right. When we ask God for miracles, we are trusting that God wants to heal our world.

And one day, when Jesus returns, God will heal everything. Every prayer for healing will be answered. Every prayer for life will be addressed. Jesus will wipe away every tear and death will be no more. This will be his ultimate intervention, his final miracle. God loves to perform miracles now because he loves to bring heaven to earth.

Do you believe that even though you may not see a miracle now, you will see the ultimate miracle when Jesus returns? Do you trust that God loves you and his creation so much that he wants to intervene in it? Can you lean on the love of Jesus enough to ask him to bring heaven to earth in your life?

NINETEEN

PROPHECY

Pursue love, and earnestly desire the spiritual
gifts, especially that you may prophesy.

—1 CORINTHIANS 14:1

Unlearn: God does not speak to me directly.

Learn: God does speak to me directly.

A WORD ABOUT WORDS

Many of us do not believe that God speaks to us directly. His voice feels far off, obscured, or bound between the covers of the Bible. But God does speak to us directly. He longs for us to experience his love by hearing his words and sharing them through prophetic words.

I understand that the mention of prophecy elicits many varied responses. Some people may respond in excitement, ready to encounter more richly a gift they already trust in and treasure. Others may be skeptical and defensive, putting their guard up against a theological unknown that seems dangerously close to the charlatan mediums on reality TV and roadside attractions. Or perhaps after making it through this book thus far, you are now on the verge of throwing it out or continuing to read it only so that you might disprove and discredit anything said in this chapter.

Trust me when I say I have responded all three ways. I will not lay out a biblical defense of the gift of prophecy in this short chapter. Contrarian, confused, or curious readers may read other books dedicated to that task. Instead, I will make the following statements to provide context for and guardrails around this divisive gateway.

1. Prophetic words are utterly subject to the Bible. If any prophetic word contradicts, undermines, deemphasizes, or questions any part of the Bible, it is to be dismissed. God never contradicts himself. Therefore, a true word from God will always be in harmony with and even amplified by the words of Scripture.

2. The gift of prophecy does not create new Scripture. While some prophecy is included in Scripture, many prophets in Israel spoke prophecies that were not included in the Bible. Just because a word is prophetic does not mean it belongs in the Bible. The canon of Scripture is closed and definitive. Nothing can or should be added to it by any prophetic word.

3. Prophetic words are not primarily predictive. The main function of the gift of prophecy, and all prophecy in general, is not to tell the future. Most of the words of the biblical prophets have nothing to do with the future but everything to do with the present. The prophets brought God's words to God's people. Occasionally, these words did include warnings of future danger, but these pale in comparison to God's voice speaking to Israel's present sin, heart, and identity. Prophets today who make much of their predictions about future events should be approached with great caution, if not outright dismissal. They are most often not carrying out the gift of prophecy but doing the very things Jesus warned us about (Matt. 24:11).

4. Practicing prophecy is commanded in the Bible. We have to take into account that Paul commanded a church under his care to eagerly desire all the spiritual gifts, especially the gift of prophecy (1 Cor. 14:1). To obey the Bible is to eagerly desire and practice the gift of prophecy. My hope is that by the end of this chapter, you won't want to pursue the gift of prophecy just because it is a command of Scripture but because you see it as a beautiful gateway God is using to teach you how to receive his love.

HEARING GOD'S HEART FOR YOU

I was in Portland, Oregon, with a group of friends from different Bible-engagement ministries around the country. We always try to kick off our hangouts together with an extended and focused time of prayer. A local church hosted us, and several of their pastors and members came to pray and listen to God alongside us. Our time began in worship, and after an extended time of prayer and silence, the members gathered around a woman from our group and began to ask God to speak to them about her. Soon it was clear that the messages people were sharing with her resonated. These strangers spoke about her identity, personality, and even things in her closet at home as if they were close friends. In tears, they wrapped up their time with her and the room fell silent again. I felt uncomfortable. I did not want them to pray over me. I did not want them to see inside the closet of my heart. Not that they would see something ugly or sinful, but I just thought they would be disappointed. I feared that God would give them a glimpse into my heart and they would all be let down at how little was there. I could hear their voices already. "That's it? Aren't you supposed to be a ministry leader? How little faith is in you! How little holiness, purity, and righteousness!" In my mind's eye I saw myself pull up the covers over my heart. I felt as though I had pulled as many blankets as possible over my head in an attempt to hide. Yet the next words out of the pastor's mouth were "Let's pray for David next." Of course.

The church members came over to me. They surrounded me, some standing and some kneeling, and laid their hands on me. The young lady who had kneeled before my chair started speaking. She said that she saw God's hand reaching into my heart and pulling the sheets back to expose me. How could she see that? She said my hands resisted and my arms were tight around the covers. But God's hands kindly prevailed and he pulled off my coverings. I couldn't believe how exposed I felt. It was as if I had told the whole room my secret thoughts. But then, to my joy, she told me what she heard God saying after he pulled off the sheets and saw me just as I am. "You are full of purity. You are exceedingly holy. You are abounding in righteousness. You are covered in goodness, fidelity, stewardship, and uprightness. God sees you fully and what he sees is very good." I wept. The lies I believed about myself fell off as I received the truth God had to say about me.

I needed God to talk directly to me. He did by speaking through a prophetic word. I was able to experience his love for me as someone carried his word to me.

This is one of the most amazing strengths the gift of prophecy offers us. We get to hear the truth of who we are to God instead of the lies of who the Enemy says we are. That is why Paul said, right after commanding the believers at Corinth to pursue the gift of prophecy, that "the one who prophesies speaks to people for their upbuilding and encouragement and consolation" (1 Cor. 14:3). Like all the gifts of the Spirit, the gift of prophecy exists to build up the church.

Prophecy is simply a human report of divine revelation. It is God's children, filled with the Holy Spirit, listening to God on another's behalf and reporting what they hear, if they've heard anything.

Often God is able to say something to us through others that we cannot receive directly ourselves. That may be because he has spoken the same words to us but we could not receive them as true because of the lies that blocked them out. It may be because we need to hear it out loud from another person rather than in the quiet of our doubting hearts. It may be because our faith needs the boost of seeing the secrets of our hearts revealed so that we might revel in how well we are known by God's all-seeing eyes. Whatever the reason, hearing God's words for us on another's lips can build up a broken-down soul like nothing else.

MART'S STORY

I was skiing in Colorado with nineteen family members when the implications of COVID-19 first hit me. I thought COVID was a problem "over there," until they shut down the mountain we were skiing on! I was oblivious to what was going on and what was about to come.

The next week, my dad asked me to be in charge of cash flow for Hobby Lobby during those uncertain times. None of us knew how long stores would be closed down. It felt as if I was thrown into a ship in Los Angeles and told not to run out of gas, but I didn't know whether the ship needed to go to San Francisco, Miami, or Hong Kong. I was overwhelmed.

By week three, a couple of miracles helped calm me down, and my song of the day was "Overcomer" by Mandisa.

By week four, the Lord started giving me ideas for how to relaunch our business. I knew we were called onward.

On Easter Sunday I wrote to seven friends I call my "adventure partners" to keep them updated and share the four Os the Lord had brought me through: from oblivious, to overwhelmed, to overcomer, and now to onward. I figured "onward" would be the last O word, but soon after sending the email, I received a response from my friend Rob Hoskins:

Mart,

Praying through this this morning, the Lord was saying you are going to do more than press onward, the Lord is positioning you for even greater things. Then he said, "You are more than conquerors, you will overachieve." This season has ensured that no one person will receive the glory or acclaim, but it will be clear to all that the Lord has done this. He has brought you through. He is the victor. He is building humility into the Green family generationally so they can bear the weight of future blessings and know that the Lord Almighty is the one that giveth and taketh away. This pruning season is to ensure healthy growth, not just in Hobby Lobby but in every member of the family who is hungry and willing to abide more deeply in him.

You will overachieve in Jesus' name,
Rob

My first thought was, *We just had nine hundred stores shut down. Overachieving sounds impossible!* All I could think of was getting the business back to somewhere near normal. I was pinching pennies and saving nickels, not dreaming of great success.

Then I went out for a run. The intensity of the previous few weeks had taken a toll, and mentally I knew it was going to be a tough run day. Plus, my time the previous week had been slow. My pace for the first few miles started to slip, and so did any remaining confidence I had. But along the way, God encouraged me, and by the end I ran my fastest time ever for a one-hour run: 7:37 a mile! Faith started to rise up in me that maybe I could overachieve not just in my running but in my family and business as well.

Rob had prophetically said I would overachieve, and so instead of feeling as though everything was a setback, I took steps forward. As it turned out, when people stayed home during the pandemic, they loved redecorating, remodeling, and reinvesting in their creative hobbies. Hobby Lobby did overachieve, with two record years back-to-back. They were our most profitable years by far, and because we give half of our profits away, God was glorified by enabling us to help more ministries than ever before in our history.

As I look back now, I was overwhelmed and just couldn't imagine overachieving. I wanted to survive, but Jesus wanted us to thrive and be a blessing to many people. He used Rob to speak to me prophetically to strengthen my faith and draw me closer to him.

GOD SPEAKS BECAUSE HE LOVES US

We learn God's love through prophetic words whether we are involved or not. We can experience his love simply because he does speak directly.

Just knowing God speaks is enough to strengthen our love for and trust in him. God speaks to us because he loves us. He speaks to us because he knows us. He speaks to us because he wants us to feel his love, know his mind, and believe who we are in him.

The fact that God would know us so personally and speak to us so specifically shatters the lies and illusions so many of us hold about God. We believe he is distant and uncaring, or waiting for us to come to him. Instead, when we believe that God is looking into our hearts and sending us messages of love through others, we learn that God is moving toward us with unrelenting, category-breaking love.

The gift of prophecy gives a double blessing. Not only does it bless and build up the person receiving the word but it also builds up the giver. God speaks to us because he is love. So when we listen to God's heart for others and share it with them, we are invited into participation with the loving heart of God.

I got to experience this joy firsthand on a trip to Uganda. I lay down to sleep on my first night after long-haul travel. As my mind slowed down, a clear picture came into view behind my closed eyes. I saw a black dress covered in bright yellow lemons. Then I heard what seemed to me a crash. I opened my eyes, sure that something had fallen in my room. When I realized nothing had happened, I closed my eyes again and saw that a crack, like in a pane of glass, had formed over the lemon dress. I heard the word *broken* and felt sadness well up in me with great force. Then the voice returned and said three times, "Do not be afraid." After the third repetition, the glass became whole and I could see the dress of lemons clearly once again. I felt in that moment that God would bring me to a woman wearing a lemon outfit during my time in Uganda and I was supposed to share this word with her.

The next day we visited a local church in Entebbe. No lemons. We visited a project we were involved with north of the city. We met many people, but none of them wore lemons. Finally, on the third day, our plans to take a break and visit the local zoo were rained out. So we shifted our plans to visit some ministry partners in the area. There at the office, I met Erika. She was wearing a stylish wide-brimmed hat, blue jeans, and a black blouse covered in bright yellow lemons.

I pulled her aside and timidly shared the picture and words with her. When I said the word *broken*, she started to cry. She told me how her husband was divorcing her. It was leaving her, her two kids, and her calling to ministry all in a state of brokenness. She had no hope and wondered if God was even paying attention to her pain. The fact that he sent me to her with a word proved that she was seen by God. I then got to pray God's heart over her. I prayed that she would not be afraid and that God would heal her brokenness.

God invited me into the story he was telling with Erika. He invited me to share in his love for and joy in Erika. He invited me to feel his compassion, act out his kindness, and embody his steadfast love. God's love became all the more real to me as I practiced prophecy with Erika. I could feel his white-hot love for this sister and how he was running after her even in her pain.

Erika needed God to talk to her directly. And God did, surprisingly, by using me. I got to carry God's love to her through a prophetic word. This made me experience the Father's heart for his children in a profound way. When we are prophesied over, we can hear God's love. When we get to prophesy over others, we get to carry God's love. When we simply observe or trust that God does use prophecy, we get to expect God's love.

Do you believe God wants to talk to you? Do you think he loves you enough to talk to others about you?

TWENTY

DREAMS

> They said to him, "We have had dreams, and there
> is no one to interpret them." And Joseph said to
> them, "Do not interpretations belong to God?
> Please tell them to me."
>
> —GENESIS 40:8

Unlearn: What I see is all that is true.

Learn: What God shows us is what is really true.

SEEING THE WORLD THE WAY GOD SEES IT

When you think about the first sermon about Jesus ever preached, what do you think it would talk about? Probably about his death and resurrection. It would most likely include claims that he was God in the flesh. It's fair to say that, given its Jewish audience, the sermon would address how Jesus fulfilled the Old Testament. All of these are correct and can be found in Peter's first sermon on the day of Pentecost (Acts 2:22–36). But most of us probably would not guess how he started his sermon—by talking about dreams and visions. Peter says, "And in the last days it shall be, God declares, that I will pour out my Spirit on all flesh, and your sons and your daughters shall prophesy, and your young men shall see visions, and your old men shall dream dreams" (Acts 2:17).

The first sermon about Jesus starts with dreams and visions.

Just as not every thought we have is a prophetic word from God, neither is every dream a message from God. The Bible sets a clear pattern that God does speak through dreams. Peter says dreams and visions will be a marker of the days following Jesus' resurrection. But that does not mean that we should try to interpret every dream or treat them all as equal. We also have to be careful how we interpret dreams. No dream from God will ever contradict Scripture or lead us to act in a way contrary to the way of Jesus.

Dreams from God typically have the following characteristics:

1. They are memorable: the details and narrative of the dream are clear and recallable (Genesis 40–41).
2. They are informative: the dream implicitly or explicitly communicates a warning, promise, command, principle, or other message (Daniel 2).

3. They are true: the dream aligns with God's Word, character, and reality (Num. 12:6).

4. They are interpretable: the dream makes sense and can be interpreted, ideally by another Christian to whom God has given the gift of dream interpretation (Dan. 2:19–28).

Dreams and visions are best understood in the context of a Christian community with a firm grasp of the Bible.

But what are dreams and visions? And why would Peter talk about them in the first gospel message the church ever preached?

Peter is quoting Scripture from the prophet Joel. In Joel's day, Israel was facing a severe famine and the threat of oncoming war. Joel talked about the day when Israel would be wiped out by her enemies. He called this the "day of the Lord." It was a day when God's justice would come on Israel for her centuries of idol worship and evil (Joel 2:1–11). Israel was in a similar state in Jesus' day. Her enemy, Rome, had taken over their land and was taxing her people into an economic famine. Many assumed they were still experiencing a "day of the Lord."

But Joel also promised another day of the Lord that would free the Israelites from their enemies and fill their homes with abundance (vv. 18–32). This would be a day of salvation not just for Israel's inhabitants but for all nations. This is the good-news day of the Lord.

It is this day of the Lord, filled with the good news of freedom, that Peter says has come. It's how he opens his whole sermon. In Joel's day and in Peter's, that great day was said to be marked by God's people having dreams and visions. But why do we need dreams and visions to see that this day of the Lord has come? Can't we behold it with our human eyes and normal waking thoughts? No.

After Jesus' resurrection, Rome was still in power. Jewish people were still oppressed. How could Jesus' disciples say that the day of the Lord had come when it seemed as if the world it promised was still a long way off? God's people needed to see reality the way God saw it. They needed a change of perspective, a look into how things actually were. Yes, to them it seemed as if Rome was in charge. But in reality God was ruling over the whole earth. Yes, they were still being persecuted by their enemies. But in reality God was working evil into good. They just couldn't see it.

What they saw was all that was true. But they needed to see the world through God's eyes to know what was really true. They needed to see the loving way God viewed them and the world through dreams and visions.

This is one of the reasons why dreams and visions exist—to show us the world the way God sees it. Here is how some Bible-nerd friends of ours describe it: "In the biblical imagination, dreams or altered states of consciousness are an in-between heaven and earth space. It's where you are able to truly encounter reality as it is, aside from all of the conscious ways that we suppress reality and rewrite reality. . . . A disarmed human mind can see reality for what it really is."[1]

How could Jewish people of Joel's day see any hope in the day of the Lord when surrounded by threats from their enemies? How could Jewish people from Peter's day see any hope in the day of the Lord when overwhelmed by the heavy hand of Rome?

---

1. Jon Collins and Tim Mackie, "Dreams and Visions," May 4, 2020, in *BibleProject Podcast*, produced by Dan Gummel, https://bibleproject.com/podcast/dreams-and-visions/.

They needed God to break through the hopelessness that filled their sight with dreams and visions of his reality. Dreams and visions are God's way of breaking through the noise of our normal way of perceiving the world to show us what is really going on.

"MY CHURCH! MY CHURCH! MY CHURCH!"

I was in college studying the Bible and biblical languages. At this point in my life I did not believe in the ongoing miraculous gifts of the Holy Spirit. I'm not saying I doubted they could happen. I was theologically convinced that God had decided to stop. Therefore, gifts such as prophecy and dreams were nonexistent for believers today. While it took my theology a while to catch up, my mind was changed forever one night during my junior year in college.

My passion for writing and performing spoken-word poetry was growing. A homeless ministry I worked with in downtown Oklahoma City asked me to write a poem for an upcoming outreach they were hosting. They wanted me to write on the theme of unity in Ephesians 5. This would be the first poem I ever wrote in response to a biblical passage (spoiler alert, that's mainly what I have done for the past fifteen years). Up to this point I had been writing poetry about social justice and causes I cared about in my city and around the world. This was different.

That night I sat down and spent hours writing until my first draft of the unity poem was done. I went to bed and had a dream that was unlike anything I had ever experienced. It was simple and recallable. It had a strong central message. It spoke directly to something in my life. It felt like an encounter with God.

In the dream, I was standing in a dark space. A spotlight hit a figure in front of me. Out of the black room a woman walked slowly toward me. She was beautiful but looked tired and worn down. Most strikingly of all, though, she was wearing a wedding dress. The dress was tattered and off-white but still gorgeous and well made. She walked right up to me, reached out toward my chest, and grabbed a handful of my shirt. Pulling me close, in a voice raspy from pain but full of love, she said, "My church! My church! My church!" Immediately, I woke up with one thought in my head. God was calling me to use the gifts he has given me, including poetry, to care for his hurting church.

God showed me his reality. He revealed to me the way he saw my life. God was giving me the opportunity to see the loving way he views the world and me.

I thought I knew who I was and what I was made for. I was a Bible nerd slash freedom fighter who would spend his days sticking it to the man. But God saw me differently. And in that dream, he peeled back my waking vision to show me his reality.

Nevertheless, I did not tell a soul. I didn't tell my roommate or my best friend. I didn't tell my girlfriend or share it with her when she became my wife. I hid that dream so well that I even began to question it. I began to trust what I saw over what God had shown me. I was losing touch with the loving way he saw me.

Over the next several years, my heart grew for the church. I wrote more and more Bible-based poems and sermons to speak to her wounds and call her to her beauty in Jesus. But after several years of skimping by and not feeling the traction I wanted, I was ready to give up. I took a band, comprising three friends, on one last poetry tour of the country. After these shows, I was done. I would turn my attention away from the church and toward other endeavors.

One of our last shows was in Kenosha, Wisconsin. Some friends hosted us in a great venue and brought a ton of their church members to the show. After we finished, they asked if their church could pray over us. Of course, we said yes. Several of the church members started to pray and it was clear that God was speaking to them about us. They were saying things about our hearts, hopes, and pasts that no one could have known, things that we desperately needed to hear from our Father. Tears were flowing and my heart was healing. Finally, one of the women came up to me and asked if she could put her hand on my chest. After I said yes, she grabbed a handful of my shirt, pulled me close, and in that same raspy love-filled voice, she said, "My church! My church! My church!"

I couldn't believe it. I began to sob as a humongous smile took over my face. The dream and all its meaning flooded back to me with a mighty force. I had lost sight of who I was and how I was made. But God showed me his vision for my life with fresh clarity. God was not going to let me walk away from his call on my life or who he made me to be. And since that day, I haven't.

This dream continues to unfold in new ways as we serve our local church and the global church through all the different opportunities God brings our way. But two of my favorite ways this dream has continued to come true happened back on the campus of my college where the dream first came.

It took me years to see the connection, but my wife and I were married in a small black box theater on our college campus. On our wedding day, as we were surrounded by blackness, a spotlight hit a beautiful woman in a wedding dress as she walked toward me. I got to marry my bride in the same environment in which God called me, in a dream, to care for his. My identity is also tied to who I am as a husband. In my waking perception of life I may think that I chose her, but this dream showed me God's reality—he chose her for me.

Second, our ministry, Spoken Gospel, filmed dozens of short films over the course of five years in that same black box theater. What for? To introduce the message and good news of every book of the Bible to God's church through spoken-word poetry. My waking eyes and normal logical patterns make it easy to think that we started it and we have to be the ones to continue to carry it. That load is heavy and the doubt and fear set in quickly. But through that vision, God showed me the reality that Spoken Gospel was his idea. We are simply living it out.

There is hardly a time when I have felt more in the center of God's loving care than when all of these connections first hit me. He used a dream to call me to his purpose, confirm who I am, and show me how he has been orchestrating it all the whole time.

If I lived my life based only on what I could see, I would miss out on so much. But through dreams and visions, God has let me see the loving way he views my life and the world.

MART'S STORY

I awoke in the middle of the night, my mind still swimming from a dream. In the dream, I was slumped over, my forehead resting on a desk, and I was crying over the word *everything*.

Later that morning as I read God's Word, there it was again in Scripture: "Jesus looked at him and loved him. 'One thing you lack,' he said. 'Go, sell everything you have and give to the poor, and you will have treasure in heaven. Then come, follow me.' . . . Then Peter spoke up, 'We have left everything to follow you!'" (Mark 10:21, 28 NIV).

That put me on high alert for the word *everything*. The next day at church, *everything* was in my pastor's sermon text, and two days later I read it another time in Scripture: "Jesus said, 'Truly I tell you, this poor widow has put more into the treasury than all the others. They all gave out of their wealth; but she, out of her poverty, put in everything—all she had to live on'" (Mark 12:43–44 NIV).

A dream, a sermon, and two verses, all in forty-eight hours. One week later my pastor started a new sermon series called "Dreamer: The Life of Joseph." He challenged us to come up with one word for the year. I wrote in my notes: "Dream—one word—everything."

Then my good friend Andy McKamie told me his wife, Rhonda, had been playing a Christian music station when a song came on that repeated the line "you give me everything" twelve times. It turned out to be the song "Everything" by Lauren Daigle. Andy told me, "I'll definitely continue praying for the picture coming together, especially in the area of risking and what God might be asking of you."

Over time, I discerned that this theme of everything is related to self-denial. Jesus called his disciples to deny themselves and take up their crosses to follow him, but often self-denial gets a bad rap. It's seen as negative. But God wanted me to see the positive side of self-denial, the side of being generous with everything.

From the world's point of view, generosity feels like losing, but from God's perspective it's freedom from the world and fruitfulness in his kingdom. In order to be generous with everything—my time, talent, treasure, trust, testimony, and thankfulness—I first had to let God lead me to choose the cross. The abundant life Jesus offers is on the other side of a cross—his cross and mine. God had a gift he wanted to give me and many gifts he wanted to give through me, but self-denial had to come first. So God sent me a dream that he confirmed with his Word and the words of others close to me.

Dreams are often mysterious and otherworldly. I don't always know how to understand them, but there are times when God uses them to speak to us in pictures things that are too deep for words.

REVEALING GOD'S REALITY

Dreams and visions show us a small picture of God's reality. They are one of God's ways of showing us what he sees. He invites people to see the loving way he views them and the world. This is their function throughout the whole Bible.

Abraham was promised a child, but he saw only infertility and old age. But God showed Abraham the reality of how many children he would have in a vision of the numberless stars (Gen. 15:1–7).

Jacob saw only the covenant promises of God as part of his swindled birthright. But, in the famous dream of Jacob's ladder, God showed Jacob that, in reality, he was chosen to receive the promises (Gen. 28:10–17).

Daniel could only see the unbeatable behemoth of Babylon that had enslaved his people. But in a series of dreams and visions, God showed Daniel the reality of Babylon's ultimate fall and God's ultimate victory (Daniel 7–12).

Mary's husband, Joseph, saw her out-of-wedlock pregnancy as a scandal to be resolved by a quiet divorce. But God showed Joseph the reality of his son's virgin birth in a dream (Matt. 1:19–25).

Ananias saw the soon-to-be apostle Paul as a murderous Pharisee to be avoided at all costs. But in a vision God showed Ananias that he would use Paul to take the gospel to the nations (Acts 9:10–16).

Peter could only see how Jesus' saving work applied to his own people, the Jews. But in a vision God showed him that he was making all nations clean (Acts 10:9–16, 34–48).

This pattern of God using dreams and visions to show people his reality occurs again and again in Scripture (Gen. 20:1–7; 28:10–17; 37:1–11; 41; 1 Samuel 3; Judg. 7:12–15; 1 Kings 3:5; Matt. 2:13; 27:19; Luke 1:5–23; Acts 16:9–10; 2 Cor. 12:1–6; Revelation).

Our perceptions of who we are, who God is, and what is going on in the world around us often cloud our vision of God's love, attention, and good plans. God's desire to lay his reality over our vision like a new pair of glasses is a deep kindness. Most people won't experience dreams from God on a regular basis, and visions appearing to our waking eyes may be even rarer. But God is using dreams and visions to share his reality with those who need it most.

A well-documented phenomenon keeps occurring in predominately Muslim countries closed to Christians and the message of Jesus. People who have never heard the gospel are seeing visions of Jesus and coming to put their trust in him. Here is one story provided by one of the largest and most well-respected Christian missions movements in the world, Lausanne:

Mohammed of northern Nigeria did not have just one dream of Jesus Christ—he had seven! Son of a prominent Fulani herdsman, Mohammed had studied the Qur'an in depth at several Muslim schools and was preparing to leave for advanced studies in Saudi Arabia when he experienced the series of dreams that convinced him of the deep love and lordship of Jesus Christ. Although his father tried to kill him in the wake of his conversion, Mohammed survived the various attempts on his life and persevered in his Christian walk, eventually leading his father to faith in Christ.[2]

God uses dreams and visions to communicate his reality to us when perhaps nothing else can. When we can't see the loving way he views us and our world, we can ask God for dreams and visions to break through and show us.

God wants to show you the world the way he sees it. He wants to reveal himself to you, even if it is through a dream. Would you receive God's love if he communicated it through a dream? Would you believe that the dream of God's love for you could really come true?

---

2. "More Than Dreams: Muslims Coming to Christ through Dreams and Visions," Lausanne World Pulse, January 2007, https://lausanneworldpulse.com /perspectives-php/595.

INVITATION TO LOVE

The most important and perhaps most difficult thing you will ever do in your life is learn to be loved by God. To grasp, believe, know, enjoy, trust, revel in, and center your identity on how perfectly you are loved by God is the great and critical work of every human being.

This is most beautifully captured in a prayer written by the apostle Paul. It was recorded in a letter he wrote to a church he planted and spent much of his ministry caring for. This is the same prayer I believe he would pray for us today.

What if one of the Bible's most prolific and influential authors prayed for you? What would he pray? What would he want for you? What would his heart's deepest desire for your life be?

I think it would be the prayer the apostle Paul wrote in Ephesians 3:14–19.

It would be a prayer about love. It is not a prayer that God would love you, for that is already the case. It is not a prayer that you would love God or others, though both will surely come to anyone who receives what this prayer requests. It's not a prayer for more love, deeper love, or truer love.

It's a prayer that you might learn to be loved.

That you, together with every other Christian, might grasp and treasure the boundless and category-breaking love God has for you.

Paul prayed this prayer because of the truth he wrote just before it. He called the truth a mystery (Eph. 3:3, 4, 6, 9) that has been hidden for ages (v. 9). But that hidden mystery is now being made known (v. 3), being revealed (v. 5), and coming into the light (v. 9). This mystery is about the unsearchable riches of Christ (v. 8). It's a mystery that could only be accomplished through God's manifold wisdom (v. 10). It's a mystery that accomplishes the eternal purposes for which God created the world (v. 11).

What is this mystery? It is that God is making all nations, all peoples, all demographics, and all cultures into his own family (v. 6). He is adopting and giving the riches of his kingdom to human beings all over the world, even those who have been his enemies. None of us are good people, and none of us are worthy candidates (2:1–3). But God is forming a global family out of us all and making us heirs of his heavenly fortune.

In short, this is the gospel. That God loved the world so much that he became flesh in his Son, Jesus, to save us from our sins, defeat our Enemy, and bring us to himself.

If you are not floored by this truth, if you are not overwhelmed with joy and confidence and gratefulness, you are not alone. That is exactly why Paul prayed. He prayed for his church and his prayer was for us, too, that we all may be able to grasp how intensely we are loved. That we might learn to be loved.

I invite you to read that prayer now. Read it slowly. Read it multiple times.

For this reason I bow my knees before the Father, from whom every family in heaven and on earth is named, that according to the riches of his glory he may grant you to be strengthened with power through his Spirit in your inner being, so that Christ may dwell in your hearts through faith—that you, being rooted and grounded in love, may have strength to comprehend with all the saints what is the breadth and length and height and depth, and to know the love of Christ that surpasses knowledge, that you may be filled with all the fullness of God. (Eph. 3:14–19)

This is my prayer for you. This is Mart's prayer for you. We pray that you would know Jesus' love for you. That God would give you the supernatural strength necessary to overcome the lies, doubts, and emotional reservations that will come against you through this process. We pray that God would root you, from the deepest parts of yourself, into his boundless and category-breaking love. We pray that you will learn to be loved.